DEVELOPING EGO FUNCTIONS IN DISTURBED CHILDREN

DEVELOPING **EGO** FUNCTIONS

IN DISTURBED CHILDREN:

Occupational Therapy in Milieu

by Lela A. Llorens and Eli Z. Rubin

LAFAYETTE CLINIC AND
WAYNE STATE UNIVERSITY

WAYNE STATE UNIVERSITY PRESS, DETROIT 1967

Lafayette Clinic Handbooks in Psychiatry, Number 1

Contents

Preface

This handbook has resulted from six years of experimental work in the development of effective milieu programming for children at Lafayette Clinic. It presents and discusses specific programs in occupational therapy which provide corrective emotional experiences for disturbed children in residential treatment. It has been written primarily for use by occupational therapists. However, the concepts and methodologies presented have already proven to be useful to other members of the child treatment team, as well as those interested in the specific therapeutic contribution of occupational therapy in the treatment of disturbed children.

Developing Ego Functions in Disturbed Children presents a method for the practice of occupational therapy in milieu treatment for emotionally disturbed children. This utilizes corrective treatment and rehabilitation approaches and discusses the contribution of occupational therapy to the total treatment of the child in the following areas: the development of adequate motor skills and coordination; the development of positive interpersonal relationships; the modification of maladaptive behavioral functioning; the development of appropriate social skills; the appropriate fulfillment of psychological and emotional needs; working through in areas of psychodynamic conflict; and re-training in areas of cognitive-perceptual-motor dysfunction through the use of graded activity programs and intensive individual work.

As in any endeavor of this kind, one becomes indebted to many people who offer assistance and encouragement. We would like to acknowledge with gratitude the contributions of several such individuals, all of Lafayette Clinic: Peter G. S. Beckett, M.D., assistant director for research, and chief, Adolescent Service; C. Donald Beall, special education teacher; Gayle Beck, head, Special Education; Abraham Elson, consultant, Child Psychiatry; Patricia Franks, staff therapist, Occupational Therapy; David Freides, chief psychologist, Adolescent Service; Shirley German, former staff therapist, Occupational Therapy; James Grisell, head, computing laboratory; Mary C. Harren, former nursing supervisor; C. David Jones, former psychiatric resident; Vivian Moore, volunteer typist; Clyde B. Simson, chief, Children's Service; Virginia Webb, occupational therapy assistant; and Erwin Wallack, former psychiatric resident.

Our sincere thanks also to Joseph P. Llorens, teacher, Detroit Public Schools.

L.A.L.
E.Z.R.

1 Overview and Rationale

The average child's personality changes as he develops. For his emotional growth to proceed in a natural and spontaneous way it must be nurtured with affection, understanding, security, and discipline, and be stimulated by achievement and social acceptance. It is necessary, too, that the child gain satisfaction in his relationships with others so that he may develop the feeling that he is lovable, that his individuality is respected, and that he can have confidence in his own strength and capability as a person. As the child develops he begins to explore his environment, establish relationships, and acquire knowledge and skills which enable him to successfully adapt to his world. If the child, however, is frustrated in his efforts to achieve mastery of himself and his environment as he strives for emotional maturity—either by lack of nurturance, lack of appropriate external stimulation, or by internal limitations—disturbances in behavior, difficulties in interpersonal relationships, and the inability to cope with stress can result. Maladjusted behavior has

9

been recognized particularly in children who are unable to make sense out of their world, or to meet the demands that the world makes on them. The child must adapt to his environment, and because of limitations within himself or those of his environment, his efforts at adaptation may be inadequate.

Some children who are unable to obtain mastery of perceptual or manipulative developmental skills are particularly vulnerable to stress in their relationships with parents, siblings, and peers. These children are unable to perform necessary functional, daily life-tasks successfully, and are unable to interact or compete in pre-school and later school activities; the concept that they subsequently develop of themselves as inadequate individuals can interfere markedly with their relationships with others.

Other children who are primarily victims of emotional and psychological trauma resulting from lack of nurturance, security, sufficient affection, consistency, and understanding can suffer overwhelming emotional conflicts and experience intense anxiety stemming primarily from interpersonal relationships. The frustration resulting from failure precipitated by the inability to get along with others, to relate to family members, to adjust at home or in the community, and to achieve in everyday living activities can result in aggressive, provocative behavior in some children; in others, such frustration may cause the child to be withdrawn and asocial. Such behavior in either case can incur derision and rejection or overprotection and overconcern from parents, and can cause the child to be excluded from cooperative play with peers and siblings. These reactions by parents and peers soon lead the child to question his adequacy and worth and contribute to feelings of low self-esteem and failure. Continued reinforcement of such negative feelings can manifest itself in intensification or generalization of maladjusted behavior.

Children who have developed maladaptive behavior and who have not achieved satisfactory emotional maturity require appropriate therapeutic intervention that will allow them to attain mastery of themselves and their environment, experience successful achievement, and develop positive interpersonal relationships. The feedback from successful interaction with objects and people provided in a corrective treatment and rehabilitation experience, such as provided in occupational therapy, often renders the child more accessible to help provided through primary psychological methods which are directed toward helping the child develop or regain feelings of self-worth and adequacy or to gain insight into his problems and understanding and acceptance of himself.

For the past several years occupational therapists have been searching intensively for greater specificity and definition of the role and function of occupational therapy in the psychiatric treatment of the emotionally disturbed child, with varying degrees of success. Occupational therapists working with this disability group have planned therapeutic activity programs to meet the needs of these children largely by experimentation, reliance on previous experience, and borrowing from the application of occupational therapy as defined for adult psychiatric patients.

Several approaches to activity programming for emotionally disturbed children have been reported in the literature. Donald L. Weston has described procedures in which activities are planned for groupings based on symptomatic behavior such as aggressivity and submissiveness. Another approach, which was developed and studied by Carl W. Fairman, utilizes activity programs aimed toward increased understanding of the dynamics of the patient's behavior through the use of projective media and toward fulfillment of the demonstrated psychological needs of the patient. Programs aimed at providing a corrective emotional experience through the use of the interpersonal relationships which are developed around mutual participation in varied activities have also been proposed.

At various times in the early years of programming for emotionally disturbed children at the Lafayette Clinic, each of these approaches has been tried in turn.* However, in the continual search for a more specific functional approach to the treatment of the emotionally disturbed child, systematic study has brought us to the use of combined treatment and rehabilitation approaches. "Treatment" means modification of psychological processes, and "Rehabilitation" means developing within the handicapped child more effective ways of coping with stress. The purpose of this handbook is to present in some detail both the theoretical and technical aspects of an occupational therapy program developed for the emotionally disturbed child, and to relate this program to its function in milieu treatment.

The children with whom this program was developed were classified as emotionally disturbed and represented such diagnostic categories as adjustment reaction of childhood, schizophrenic reaction, personality disorders, psychoneurotic disorders, and chronic brain syndrome. For the purposes of specific and appropriate programming it was recognized that the psychological needs of the children must be understood as well as their functional capabilities and behavioral reactions, regardless of diagnostic classification. It was also recognized that the methodology proposed to meet the children's needs, to modify func-

* Lafayette Clinic is a research, training, and short-term intensive treatment facility for psychiatric illness. Twenty-two of its 145 beds are devoted to residential care of emotionally disturbed children.

tional limitations, and to develop the children's potentials should be related to the techniques and media available to the occupational therapist.

Recognition of these factors resulted in the acceptance of the continuum of developmental functions in its various aspects—physical, intellectual, social, and emotional—as the model upon which to build an approach to programming in occupational therapy that would develop and improve ego functions needed by the child to cope effectively with everyday life situations. Programming based on such an approach helps the child achieve successful mastery of himself and his environment through his own efforts by standards appropriate to his developmental level, and are therefore meaningful to him. It is felt that such an approach aids the child in building those skills which will help him toward more successful adaptation in social, psychological, and intellectual areas. This approach involves progressive, graded planning and implementation. Programming begins with evaluation of the child's level of functioning in areas of physical skills, behavioral characteristics, and capacity to relate to others. Placement in a group is based on the child's demonstrated ability to perform in certain physical skills, his capacity to relate to others, and his ability to control his own behavior. The child is placed in that group within the program which specifically provides the activities and expectation around behavior and performance commensurate with his current capacities, and where the opportunities for immediate success in the area of primary need are present. A gradual increase in expectation of him, both in performance and behavioral control with the support for independent functioning that is necessary for emotional growth to take place, is provided through the several steps in the program. Flexibility in programming is maintained to allow for individual differences in children, but the sequence is arranged so that children can build on previously learned as well as newly acquired skills as they move toward more adequate, independent functioning.

This program is based on findings of a study by the current authors which indicated that through the use of a directed teaching approach and activities aimed at helping the child achieve mastery through learning and practice, significant changes in the child's performance in skilled activities and behavioral adjustment could be seen in a relatively short time. Empirical data and further study support our impressions that this approach offers a more specific contribution to the overall treatment of the disturbed child, particularly in a setting which subscribes to the milieu therapy concept. It is a natural approach which offers the child opportunity, incentive, and the necessary support to grow emotionally and achieve greater ego development.

Attention is paid to developing both the physical and adaptive skills as well as social competence, with the implicit recognition that the increase in his capacity to cope successfully with the demands of the environment will allow the child to enjoy more meaningful social interaction. In this way the child is motivated not only by the positive response feedback from others but, more importantly, he experiences personal satisfaction from his successful achievement. The immediate goals of the program are to increase the child's level of functioning in the area of visual motor skill and coordination to a point commensurate with that expected for his age, to increase his capacity to relate to others, and his ability to control his own behavior. Reduction of stress associated with expectations for achievement at a level higher than that of which the child is capable, is often sufficient to allow the child to begin to experience success in areas in which he has previously failed, thus interrupting the pattern of repeated failures which disturbed children often encounter.

Psychological needs for love and affection, the feeling of belonging, expression of aggression, discipline, and dependency gratification are met chiefly through interpersonal relationships; however, fulfillment of the need to feel adequate, worthy, and able to achieve successfully is obtained only partially through approval from others. The individual also develops a concept of his own worth through the feedback he receives from the experiences he has in his environment while striving for and achieving mastery of objects and self. Successful achievement in all areas of function are necessary for the development of a mature personality and effective coping behavior.

2 Milieu Treatment Planning

Lafayette Clinic subscribes to milieu therapy as a necessary complement to individual psychotherapy in the treatment of all psychiatric patients. In the treatment of disturbed children, the milieu is particularly important as much of the child's life work is carried on in the environment of the school as well as in social situations. In a psychiatric milieu all of the patient's experiences will effect him, either positively or adversely. Few experiences will be neutral. Many of the patient's reactions will be based on his previous experiences, others will be the result of new learning in the form of positive, health-stimulating experiences in a therapeutic milieu. Milieu refers to environment. Milieu therapy is defined as the planned manipulation of the environment aimed at producing changes in the personality of the patient. In this book we use the term "milieu" to designate the total environment of the emotionally disturbed child in residential treatment, and describe it here to provide a better understanding of how the occupational therapy program fits into the total scheme.

The physical aspects of the milieu consist of the living unit or ward, the school, the occupational therapy area, the industrial shop, the gym, and the playground.

Programs in each of these areas contribute specifically to the overall treatment, habilitation, or rehabilitation of the child.

The Ward

The ward program offers a well-organized environment which is comfortable and supportive, using as treatment media the activities and natural routines of daily living which are supervised by adults who are capable of establishing relationships with others and understanding individual differences. The staff-to-patient ratio of 1:4 during the active part of the child's day provides ample opportunities for interaction with adult authority figures who are consistent, understanding, and benign. Peer interaction under adult supervision and control is used to support an acceptable social role for each member of the group. As substitute parents, nursing personnel strive to fulfill basic physical and psychological needs. The living atmosphere avoids overstimulation and provides for redirection as well as constructive and appropriate channelling of energies.

The School

The main objective of the residential school is to help the child develop and maintain positive attitudes toward the various aspects of school and to progress in his aca-

17

demic skills so that he will experience minimum delay in his education due to placement in residential treatment. Through assessment of the strengths and weaknesses in academic skills or readiness for school activities, individualized programs of instruction are planned to reduce the stress so often associated with school adjustment. The child is helped to fill in existing gaps in his academic skills, knowledge, or achievement through individual remedial instruction and small classes. Appropriate school behavior is patterned through the use of structure and limit-setting. Such instruction and patterning enables the child to become better prepared to cope with the demands of school on his return to the community.

Occupational Therapy

The occupational therapy program provides a setting, activities, and interpersonal relationships through which the child can increase his mastery of objects and management of his body as well as acquire appropriate social skills and behavioral control.

Industrial Arts

The industrial arts program supplements the occupational therapy program for those children who have the necessary capabilities to participate successfully in activities which require more complex planning and more adequate skills. Wood is used here as the media of therapy. Self-organization and self-control are further developed in this program.

Recreational Therapy

Recreational therapy programming contributes to the development of recreational and social skills. Increased feelings of adequacy are achieved through successful interaction with others in planned activities. New skills

18

are learned, adequate skills involving gross motor control are developed, and opportunities for cooperative group participation are provided.

GENERAL ATTITUDES

In addition to the specific programming offered by each of the disciplines within the milieu, there are other factors which contribute to the overall therapeutic management of the child. The appropriate attitudes and methods of discipline used with each child must be consistent to be effective, and therefore emphasis is placed on the consistency of both the methods of discipline and the use of appropriate attitudes with each child among all who come in daily contact with him.

The literature, as well as experience, has given us some clues regarding general attitudes most effective with disturbed children. A close look at the records from the ward, school, occupational therapy, and recreational therapy reveal the following general attitudes:

Understanding of the child and the particular problems he manifests in each respective area. Both formal and informal methods of assessment and communication regarding the child's areas of strength and weakness should be used to enable the staff to maintain an objective, rational, non-stressful approach.

Acceptance, consistent with the child's current capacities, considering both assets and potentials as well as the limitations that the child demonstrates.

Supportive of the goals of treatment set forth by each discipline which are based on full awareness and understanding of the overall treatment goals for the individual child.

Consistency, both among the various members of the staff and within the same person at different times, thus providing the kind of stability and reliability which encourages a sense of trust within the child.

Morally non-judgmental toward the child who needs to express primitive impulses or display attitudes considered socially unacceptable, and with the recognition of the need for limit-setting and re-direction.

These general attitudes must be individualized considerably and delineated concretely to meet the specific needs of individual children.

Behavior Management

Discipline which is necessarily employed with the immediate goal of controlling the child's behavior must have as its eventual goal helping the child learn to control his own behavior. To accomplish this, it is not enough just to limit the behavior, the child must know why the behavior is unacceptable as well as learn ways which are acceptable.

Following are guide lines found useful in the management of aggressive, acting-out behavior:

1. Define the boundaries of the limits to the child, delineating what behavior will be permitted, what behavior will be tolerated, and what behavior will be controlled.

2. Define the purpose for the boundary and explain why certain kinds of behavior will be controlled—it will hurt him or hurt someone else.

3. Keep limits consistent, clear, and reasonable.

4. Avoid seducing children into behavior which is unacceptable by suggestion, such as "I know you won't be able to listen," or by introducing forbidden objects into the child's environment.

5. Restate and enforce the limits as often as necessary. The child gains immeasurable benefit from the adult who supports his compliance with the defined limit. The in-

evitable, immediate resulting feelings of resentment, hostility, or surprise form the basis for building a positive relationship between the child and the adult.

The pattern leading to eventual control of his own behavior will begin with the child ultimately accepting the fact that limits can be placed on his behavior by the environment without loss of psychological need fulfillment. Failing to supply such discipline causes the child to lose the respect for his environment and increase his feelings of guilt and anxiety. With appropriate discipline and support from the adults around him, the child can learn to internalize the limits and gain the ability to exert self-control even when an adult is not present. At such a point, failure to control will cause the child to anticipate with dread the loss of respect and support from the environment, or increase his feelings of guilt or anxiety regarding retribution.

Following are intervention techniques used successfully as needed in helping the child learn to control his behavior:

1. Planned ignoring: ignoring unacceptable behavior which may be tolerated but not approved, in such a way that the behavior is discontinued from lack of attention paid to it.

2. Proximity or touch control: sitting next to the child or touching him on the shoulder or arm may be enough to control certain kinds of behavior.

3. Extra attention and affection: giving reassurance, attention, and affection before the child finds it necessary to behave unacceptably to receive the attention and affection he desires.

4. Extra help over a difficult situation: clarifying the situation for the child, using the situation to help the child develop insight and realize why things went wrong and what might be done to avoid a recurrence.

5. Restructuring the activity or situation: removing gadgets and other objects which seduce the child into unacceptable behavior; changing the activity for the child if it is too stimulating, too difficult, or too boring; and removing the child from situations contributing to unacceptable behavior.

6. Direct appeal: appealing to the child's sense of fairness and his responsibility as a member of a group.

Considerable emphasis has been placed upon techniques helpful in the management of the child who exhibits poor impulse control. For the child who is overcontrolled, fearful, inhibited, or withdrawn a different emphasis is indicated in some areas. The following have proven helpful:

1. Provide the child with a benign setting and easily available protective adults.

2. Reduce stress of competition and expectation beyond the child's level of competence.

3. Provide structure and routine initially. A gradual decrease of such structure may be introduced as the child is able to tolerate it.

4. React in a non-judgmental manner to behavior and attitudes displayed by the child.

5. Avoid a too-close affectional relationship by personnel initially.

Treatment Planning

Besides the experiences the child receives in the milieu, he also receives individual psychotherapy, group psychotherapy, or pharmacotherapy as indicated. The psychotherapist is responsible for the overall treatment of the child; therefore, adequate communication between the psychotherapist and those responsible for implementing milieu programs is important.

To reach a treatment plan for a child which utilizes the unique contributions of individual departments, it is necessary to extract and coordinate certain essential information available from each discipline. In this setting we have found the following types of formal conferences useful in accomplishing the aim of achieving consistency in staff reactions, attitudes and behavior, and in maintaining a well-informed milieu staff. (The format for some of these conferences, as well as outlines used for reporting by various disciplines, are in Appendix A.)

Pre-admission Conference. A conference is held prior to each child's admission to the hospital. Information regarding the nature of the child's presenting problems, the character of the family constellation, and the developmental history is recorded. Other available pertinent data, such as psychological testing results, information regarding previous school performance, and precautions are also recorded. This conference is attended by representatives from Nursing, Social Service, and Psychiatry and is conducted by the chief of Children's Service. The information from the conference is available from Nursing to all the milieu therapy staff (see Appendix A).

Diagnostic Conference. A diagnostic conference is held regarding each child approximately six to eight weeks after admission to delineate and clarify further the nature of the child's problem, to formulate a diagnosis, discuss etiology, and to define the course of treatment. In this conference as well as in the progress conferences, the interdisciplinary staff conference, and review rounds, certain specific information is reported by each discipline. From the school information regarding the child's level of academic functioning, his academic assets, and limitations his behavioral adjustment in school and his characteristic ways of dealing with problem areas which arise in the pursuit of academic achievement are reported. From occupational therapy information concerning the child's motor skills and coordination, his behavioral reactions in this situation, characteristic ways of dealing with frustration, tolerance of others, and his ability to form relationships are reported. Information regarding the child's social skills, gross motor skills, and abilities to interact in group activities is reported by the recreational therapy department, while nursing reports information concerning the child's skills in the activities of daily living, his behavioral reactions in this situation, and his ability to relate to adults and other children.

There is considerable overlap in the areas of observation of a child's behavior as reported by the various disciplines in the milieu, such that more than one observation of a child's reaction to frustration, ability to relate, and other behavioral reactions is available.

Social service contributes an understanding of the environment in which the child developed through family history information. The clinical psychologist provides information regarding the intellectual, perceptual, and psychological functioning of the child, as well as information which contributes to increased understanding of the dynamics of the child's emotional maladjustment. The psychotherapist contributes an understanding of the psychosexual development and psychodynamics presented by the child, coordinates and directs milieu treatment, and conducts intensive psychotherapy and pharmacotherapy as indicated.

Each of the disciplines represented utilizes information from the others in the establishment of continuing treatment plans supportive to the overall plan, utilizing those techniques and procedures unique to it.

Progress Conference. These are held regarding each

child at approximately eight week intervals to review changes in the child's functioning—behaviorally, socially, psychologically, and academically.

Interdisciplinary Staff Conference. This is held as a follow-up to the diagnostic and progress conferences. It is attended by representatives from Nursing, Special Education, Occupational Therapy, and Recreational Therapy and chairmanship of the meeting rotates among the participants. The purpose of this conference is to discuss the treatment recommended for the patient by the diagnostic and progress conferences. Each discipline interprets and implements the recommendations using those techniques and media unique to it.

Review Rounds. A weekly review is held for the purpose of communicating on-going behavior, changes, and problems which occur regarding the management of the children, as well as for communicating changes, or anticipated changes, regarding the treatment planning for the children. Representatives from all disciplines attend this conference.

Coordination Conference. This is held bi-weekly for the purpose of facilitating communication and coordination regarding the scheduling of milieu therapy programs, as well as special activities and events. This meeting is attended by representatives of the milieu staff and is conducted by the head of the Division of Rehabilitation.

Ward Conference. This is held weekly for members of the nursing staff and is conducted by the ward administrator. Its purpose is to facilitate communication regarding the behavior and relationships of the children specific to the living unit.

Such a comprehensive approach to treatment planning for the disturbed child provides an atmosphere which contributes maximally to his treatment. It provides consistency, stability, and predictability in the environment and individual experiences necessary for the child in daily living tasks, specific perceptual and motor tasks, academic learning, and opportunities for success.

3 Evaluation and Treatment Planning

The function of occupational therapy in this setting includes: evaluation, treatment, and rehabilitation. An evaluation of the patient in the areas of skill, behavior, and his ability to relate to others is essential; it provides information which allows the occupational therapist to make an independent contribution to the diagnostic work-up of each patient, as well as providing useful information from which the occupational therapist can plan meaningful treatment and rehabilitation programs for the handicapped child.

GRADED ACTIVITY PROGRAM

The core activity program consists of three groups: The basic skills group, the intermediate group, and the advanced group.* The total group of children range in

---

* This group was called the average skills group in "A Directed Activity Program for Disturbed Children," *American Journal of Occupational Therapy,* XVI (1962), 287.

age from six to twelve years and represent a variety of psychiatric diagnostic categories. The size of groups varies according to the population; however, eight is the maximum that can be effectively worked with per group at a given time. Groupings are effected through consideration of the level of each individual child's skills, the degree of structure and guidance he needs, and his capacity for self-control.

The basic skills group is designed for children ranging in age from six to twelve but who are functioning at a level equivalent to seven or below. The emphasis is initially placed on patterning behavior, developing adequate interpersonal relationships, and increasing or maintaining visual motor skills. Children who are over seven and who demonstrate a level of skills, behavior, or ability to relate to others that is markedly below that expected for their respective ages would be placed in this group, along with children who are chronologically six and seven. Some of the maladaptive behavior characteristics which may be present in these children, regardless of age, are short attention span, distractibility, low frustration tolerance, hyperactivity, poor impulse control, and autistic preoccupation. In their relationships with others they may demonstrate overaggressiveness or extreme inhibition and withdrawal; they may be overly dependent or ambivalently independent. Their primary needs in the areas of skill would be to increase visual awareness and to develop adequate coordination and motor control. The activities used initially with this group are structured, repetitive, and minimally stimulating.

The intermediate group is designed for children from eight to twelve years. The emphasis is initially placed on continued increase of motor skills and coordination, the development of adequate interpersonal relationships, and appropriate patterns of behavior. Children who are ten or older are placed in this group when the level of their skills, behavior, or ability to relate is judged to be somewhat below that expected for their respective ages. Some of the behavior characteristics which may be demonstrated by this group include distractibility, restlessness, inadequate attention span, and immaturity. In their relationships with others they may lack knowledge of appropriate modes of relating with peers, may be shy or aggressive, and may be suspicious and distrusting of adults. The specific needs of this group in the area of skills would be further practice and opportunity for mastery in visual motor skills and coordination. The activities for this group are both structured and expressive.

The advanced group is designed primarily for ten to twelve year olds. The emphasis is initially placed on maintaining the level of the child's visual motor skill and coordination, developing appropriate attitudes toward and modes of assuming independence, developing self-reliance as well as group identification and appropriate interpersonal relationships. The children in this group have adequate skills relative to those expected for their ages, adequate interest, good motivation, attention span, and frustration tolerance and have the capacity to develop self-organization and assume constructive independence. The activities for the advanced group are craft-oriented. The program is structured and is presented in units; however, within each unit there is opportunity for creativity, self-organization, and independent functioning.

The several steps in this program are designed to provide incentive for growth within its structure. The activities for each group are specific to that group; overlapping is avoided as much as possible. The children can then strive to "graduate" to the next group and know what to expect when this is achieved. The approach used is to begin the child's activities at the level and in the group in which he can function successfully and gradually increase the difficulty and complexity of the activities. The attitude of the occupational therapist is supportive, with encouragement for independent decision making and problem solving.

The role of the occupational therapist in the group is that of an enabler. The enabler helps the group learn new ideas and develop new skills. The occupational therapist is active in the initial direction of an activity, acquainting the children with the techniques involved n acquiring a particular skill. He then becomes less and less active as the child practices the skill and moves toward mastery.

The placement of a child in one of the three groups is primarily contingent upon his achievement on the evaluation battery. However, flexibility must be maintained to provide the most effective corrective experience for the child. Several combinations of scores can be achieved on the evaluation battery and each combination has a corresponding place in the activities program.

EVALUATION FOR O.T. PROGRAMMING

To evaluate the level of a child's skills a simple battery of tasks is administered shortly after the child is admitted to the hospital and observations of the child's behavior and ability to relate are made. Three tasks are used to assess: fine motor control, eye-hand coordination, and ability to integrate parts into a whole non-verbal integration) (see Appendix B).*

---

* The activities used in this battery were selected for their face validity, that is, their resemblance to actual activities that children ordinarily engage in, in occupational therapy.

Procedure for Evaluation

For the evaluation in Occupational Therapy the child is brought to the O.T. area and given a brief tour. The workroom and playroom are pointed out and a cupboard with his name on it is shown to the child. He is then seated at a worktable where materials for the evaluation have been laid out. The activity program is described in a general way, and it is explained to the child that we are interested in having him begin in a group that will be best for him and that we want to get to know him better. It is pointed out that the activities we are asking him to do in this session are similar to some of the things done by other children in the O.T. groups. Also, that the projects he makes in this session will be kept by us but subsequently he will be able to keep the things he makes and do whatever he likes with them. The following activities are presented to the child and observations made:

L-R Fine Motor Control Test: The child is given the worksheet for this test and is asked to identify each of the forms—"Tell me what you would call this," pointing to the circle, then to the square, and so on down the page. He is told to reproduce each of the forms as accurately as he can three times in the spaces provided. No time limit is imposed.

Eye-Hand Coordination Test: The child is given a 9″ x 12″ sheet of construction paper and three 4″ x 5″ sheets of paper in assorted colors. He is also given two sizes of circle patterns to trace and scissors, paste, and pencils. He is asked to trace as many circles as he can on the small colored paper, cut them out as carefully as he can, and paste them down on the larger sheet of background paper arranging them into a picture or design.

Puzzle: The child is given a thirty-piece jigsaw puzzle (four to eight year level) and asked to take it apart and assemble it. The time it takes the child to complete the puzzle, the manner in which he organizes the task, and the methods used to accomplish it are recorded.

Behavior Observations: While the child is working during the session, observations are made in the following areas: attention span, ability to concentrate, ability to follow verbal instructions, degree of motor activity, relatedness to the therapist, dependence-independence, and affect and mood.

Scoring

L-R Fine Motor Control Test*: The geometric form worksheet is given five separate scores. The circle and square are scored together, the diamond and the composite form are scored separately, and the vertical lines and the horizontal figures are scored together. The items are scored for control with which the form was reproduced. Two of the three forms produced must meet the scoring criteria to be considered for the higher of two possible scores.

Eye-hand Coordination Test: Only the child's ability to cut on a line is specifically scored on this task. The items are scored on the basis of the smoothness and accuracy of the child's cutting.

Puzzle: The time it takes the child to complete the puzzle, the manner in which he organizes the task, and the methods he uses to accomplish the task are considered in the scoring.

Behavior Scale: Descriptive terms have been used to minimize subjectivity.

Because this test was developed for the purpose of determining the functional level of a child's skills and behavior along a developmental continuum, the scoring was initially determined by theoretical developmental

* The inter-rater reliability corelation for this test is .84.

criteria from immature or undeveloped through developing to mature or well-developed functional ability. Scores of 1, 2, and 3 represent these categories. One equals inadequate, immature, or undeveloped skill and ability from a developmental point of view (samples of reproductions which would earn a score of 1 on the fine motor control and eye-hand coordination tasks may be found in Figures 4 and 5 of Appendix B). Two equals transitional or developing skill and ability and 3 equals mature or well-developed skill or ability (samples of reproductions which would earn a score of 2 may be found in Figures 6 and 7; 3 in Figures 8 and 9). Tables for scoring non-verbal integration and behavior are presented in Figures 10 and 11. The criteria for the scale are based on observation of classroom behavior of public school children. The criteria for scoring the puzzle were derived from experience with a small sample of children whose performance indicated that an eight-year old child can successfully complete this task in seven minutes or less.

The scores the child receives on the entire battery are recorded on a scoring sheet (see Figure 12). The total maximum score possible for the complete battery is 45. This score could be achieved only if the child's functioning is adequate in all areas of skill, behavior, and his ability to relate to others.

The range of scores which a child can achieve in the evaluation of his skills is 0–24. A score of 0 could be achieved only if the child was totally unable to perform the tasks. A score of 24 could be achieved if the child performed at an adequate or mature level on all tasks.

The range of possible scores in the evaluation of behavior is 4–12. Four represents inadequate or maladaptive behavioral functioning; 12 represents adequate functioning in the areas of behavior that are specifically observed.

In evaluating the child's ability to relate to others, the range of possible scores is 3–9. A score of 3 denotes inadequacy in this ability; 9 denotes adequate ability in this area.

A range of scores has been determined as representative of inadequate, transitional, and adequate functioning in the areas of skill, behavior, and relatedness based on normative data gathered with this technique. These scores are presented in Table 1.

	Skills	*Behavior*	*Relatedness*
Inadequate	0–10	4–6	3–4
Transitional	11–19	7–10	5–7
Adequate	20–24	11–12	8–9

Table 1. Range of Scores Based on Performance of Public School Children

Various combinations of scores may be earned by the individual child depending on his performance in each area represented on the evaluation battery. These variations will influence his placement in the activities program. For example, if a child achieves a score ranging from 0–10 in skills, 4–6 in behavior, and 3–4 in relatedness, he would be placed in the basic skills group, a group designed to provide practice in perceptual-motor skills, patterning of behavior, and developing appropriate social interaction, since these scores indicate that the child performs at an inadequate level in skills, behavior, and ability to relate. A second child may achieve scores ranging from 0–10 in skills, 11–12 in behavior, and 8–9 in ability to relate. These scores would indicate, as seen in Table 1, that this child is functioning at an inadequate or immature level in skills with adequate or mature functioning in behavior and ability to relate. As can be seen in Table 2, this child would also be placed in the basic skills group.

Group	Skills	Behavior	Relatedness
Basic Skills Group	0–10	4–6	3–4
	0–10	4–6	5–7
	0–10	7–10	5–7
	0–10	11–12	8–9
	11–19	4–6	3–4
	11–19	7–10	3–4
	11–19	4–6	5–7
	20–21	4–6	3–4
Intermediate Group	11–19	7–10	5–7
	11–19	11–12	8–9
	11–19	11–12	5–7
	11–19	11–12	8–9
	20–24	7–10	5–7
	20–24	11–12	5–7
	20–24	7–10	8–9
Advanced Group	20–24	11–12	8–9

Table 2. Range of Scores Affecting Group Placement

With experience, additional observations and information are available to the therapist from this evaluation battery which are useful both in evaluation and treatment. For instance, in identifying the geometric forms, the level of the child's response will yield gross information about the child's conceptual thinking. Does he call the circle a circle, a ball, or a sphere; does he call the square, a box, or a cube; is the composite shape called a circle inside of a square inside of a triangle, or is it a tent or a house; are the wiggly lines just wiggly lines or are they rain, a snake, waves, or are they lines with angles and curves? Form reversals may be produced by some children, indicating the possibility of visual perception difficulty and problems in left-right orientation. In placing his cut-out circles on the background paper, the child's imaginativeness or lack of it can be observed. The restriction or expansiveness with which the child executes the tasks may give some indication of the child's level of psychological functioning. These observations are not specifically scored nor are they fixed at various age levels.

This evaluation battery is not an intelligence test or a neurological examination, nor can it be used as a substitute for sound clinical judgment. It has been designed specifically to assess a child's functioning so that he may be appropriately placed in a graded activity program.

Because of the many adjustments a child must make to his placement in a hospital, we have found that a child who is eligible for the advanced group will adjust better if he is first placed in the intermediate group for at least two weeks.

Individualized Treatment Programs

After the child is placed in a group most appropriate to his functioning, consideration is then given to his individual psychological, social, and achievement needs; to individualize treatment within the group, it is necessary to utilize information from other sources. Such information would include the reasons for which the child was referred for psychiatric treatment; developmental history data, available from the social history; information regarding the child's psychological adjustment, his characteristic modes of behavior, his potentiality for change, available from psychological testing; and an assessment of the child from a dynamic point of view as well as his characteristic social behavior, available from psychiatry.

In this setting the reasons for referral and a description of the child's behavior are available on admission. The other information used is reported at the diagnostic conference and is available on request from each of the disciplines concerned prior to the conference.

Information from the initial evaluation is used to formulate the initial goals to be pursued in occupational therapy. These goals may, however, be revised prior to the diagnostic conference on the basis of observation of the child in the group. These initial goals formulate the basis of the treatment plan for the child during his first six weeks in O.T.

Following the diagnostic conference, the information reported by each discipline is reviewed and a continuing O.T. plan is formulated. This plan will incorporate the findings and recommendations of the conference. Subsequent changes in the plan will result from periodic re-evaluation in the O.T. group and review of the findings and recommendations reported at progress conferences.

PROGRAM PLANNING

The occupational therapy program plan for a child begins with his placement in a group or individual sessions. Following are the initial and continuing treatment goals and program plans for eight children as formulated by the occupational therapist, for use as a guide to treatment.

Case 1. Bobby A., an eleven-year old.

Description of child: Bobby was referred to Lafayette Clinic because of lateness and poor school attendance. poor peer relationships, stealing, assault & battery, and escape from the group placement center where he was living.

Social history: Bobby's mother, forty-five years old, became mentally ill when Bobby was five, has since been committed to a state mental hospital, and was reported to be depressed during her pregnancy with Bobby. His father seemed overwhelmed by the many problems that Bobby, his mother, and an older brother fifteen years old —who also had emotional problems—presented.

CLINICAL FINDINGS

Psychologcal testing revealed that Bobby was of average intelligence, full scale I.Q. 91, verbal 82, performance 103, with passive-aggressive personality traits, poor impulse control, a poor self-image, and unmet dependency needs, who handles his anxiety by denial, projection, and aggressive acting-out. Masculine sexuality was particularly threatening to him. Neurological examination was negative and his EEG was reported to show dysrythmia grade 1, non-specific. The psychiatric formulation resulted in a diagnosis of personality disorder, passive-aggressive type. Bobby was seen as an anxious, fearful child with a repetitious characterological problem and low self-esteem. His chief defenses were denial and projection. He would act out easily in an aggressive manner when anxious. The sexual area appeared to be particularly stressful. Bobby needed structure in his environment; he liked schedules and liked to plan his days at least one week ahead.

Observations from the milieu: In the ward Bobby was restless, overactive, and provocative with peers. He usually won at games and was proud of this ability. In school he was functioning from the appropriate grade level for his age to one and a half years below.

O.T. EVALUATION AND PLAN

Initial evaluation: Bobby demonstrated transitional to adequate visual motor skills and eye-hand coordination on initial evaluation in O.T. He related easily to the O.T. but seemed somewhat shy. His frustration tolerance for the testing situation was fair. He tended to project blame on the project or others when he anticipated failure. He followed verbal directions well. Bobby received the following scores: skills—18, behavior—12, relatedness—9. He was placed in the intermediate group with the goals of: establishing a relationship, providing opportunity for positive peer interaction, and activities commensurate with his level of abilities. Further observation in the O.T. group revealed transitional to adequate skills but inadequate performance. His attention span was adequate but he tended to be excessively motivated to finish first. His relationships were superficial and evidence of low self-esteem could be seen.

Continuing plan and goals: From the information available it could be seen that Bobby needed to have his dependency needs gratified, to control his aggressive acting-out behavior, to accept some mistakes gracefully, to increase his feelings of adequacy and self-esteem, and to accept responsibility for his own behavior. He also needed positive male identification.

The O.T. plan for Bobby was aimed at meeting these needs and the goals established were:
1. Use relationship to gratify dependency needs.
2. Provide consistent limits and structure to help increase impulse control.
3. Provide activities at his level of functioning for success feedback to increase feelings of adequacy.
4. Later, help him learn to realistically accept his assets and limitations, accept some mistakes and failures in his activities which would be reality-based.
5. Provide opportunities for peer interaction with clarification of his role in provocative behavior and projection of blame.

At the point at which Bobby could assume more responsibility for his own behavior and relate more appropriately with peers, he would be moved into the advanced group. The goals would then be to encourage appropriate independent functioning, self-direction, and appropriate social behavior. Placement in the industrial arts program would also be recommended at this time to reinforce masculine identification.

Case 2. Steve R., a seven-year old.

Description of child: Steve was referred to the clinic because of withdrawn behavior and habit disorder (enuresis and encopresis).

Social history: His mother. twenty-eight, was described as anxious and hostile with strong feelings of inadequacy and worthlessness which she acted-out by attempted suicide. The parents were separated but the father was said to be interested in the children. There were two other children in the family, both of whom had been frequently placed in boarding homes due to the parents' periodic inability to take care of them.

CLINICAL FINDINGS

Psychological testing revealed that Steve was of average intelligence, I.Q. 103, was withdrawn, immature, and threatened by lack of structure. No cognitive-motor dysfunction was present. The psychiatric formulation resulted in a diagnosis of personality disorder, passive-aggressive type, with special symptom reaction. Structure and limit-setting for control of impulsive behavior were recommended.

Observations from the milieu: In the ward Steve preferred solitary play and was a poor loser in group games. He also preferred to direct other children. His habit disorder continued. In school his skills were at or above grade level in all areas. His behavior alternated from resistive and impulsive to cooperative, well-motivated, and appropriate.

O.T. EVALUATION AND PLAN

Initial evaluation: Steve demonstrated transitional to adequate visual motor skills and coordination on initial evaluation in O.T. He was resistive and negative toward the first task in the evaluation battery and refused to cooperate. The second task was offered and he accepted. After completing this he accepted the one he previously refused. He gradually appeared to relax and took pleasure in what he was doing. Initially, he seemed afraid of the O.T. He held his head down and looked up through his bangs in a sullen manner. He gradually warmed up as the session progressed. His attention span was adequate. He received scores of 15 in skills, 8 in behavior, and 3 in relatedness. He was placed in the basic skills group with the goals of: establishing a relationship, providing activities appropriate to his level of functioning and opportunities for appropriate social relationships.

Further observation in O.T. revealed that Steve was self-reliant and had strong needs to control his environment. Negativism and resistance continued to be observed; however, he was more cooperative with the demands made on him when he was allowed to have an area he could control. (Care of animals was used in O.T. Care of plants was subsequently used in school. As he became more comfortable, he spontaneously gave these up.)

Continuing plan and goals: On the basis of this information, the initial O.T. goals were retained. The following were added:

1. Assist child in dealing with needs to control by giv-

ing him appropriate responsibilities within his capabilities.

2. Provide appropriate structure, consistency, and limit setting for control of impulsive behavior.

Because Steve was seven years old, he was appropriately placed in the basic skills group and would remain there.

Case 3. Laura L., a six-year old.

Description of child: Laura was referred to Lafayette because of temper tantrums, peculiar jerking movements of her extremities, peculiarity of gait, learning difficulty, and nervousness. She was described as always having had poor attention span, poor impulse control, and a tendency to withdraw from others.

Social history: Laura's family was described as indigent. Her mother was thirty-nine and described as depressed; she had a history of emotional disturbance and had received electroconvulsive therapy and pharmacotherapy. Laura's father was also thirty-nine and was described as passive-aggressive. He had suffered stomach difficulties and nervousness. He was suspected of being seductive with Laura, relating to his two sons in a hostile, arrogant manner. The eldest boy was hospitalized with a diagnosis of organic brain syndrome with behavior problems. A younger boy reportedly had poor peer relationships and stole. Neither parent saw too much wrong with Laura, although the mother felt there must be something wrong since she often fell and had severe tantrums. Both parents were described as inadequate, dependent, and overwhelmed by their problems.

CLINICAL FINDINGS

Psychological testing revealed that Laura was of border line intelligence, I.Q. 79, was disorganized and hyperactive, had no effective ego resources, and her view of reality was distorted. Her affect was described as flat and her thinking as primary process. Neurological examination was normal as was the EEG. The psychiatric formulation resulted in a diagnosis of childhood schizophrenia with autism. She was described as a child with primary process thinking, bizarre motor behavior, and inappropriate affect, who was the product of an inadequate home environment where she may have been sexually stimulated by her father and had identified with her mentally ill mother. Patterning experiences, structure, and reality-orientation were recommended. The prognosis was seen as poor and it was felt that long-term hospitalization would be needed.

Observations from the milieu: In the ward Laura tiptoed, twirled, talked to herself in the mirror, grimaced, growled, and was incoherent. She enjoyed playing in the sandbox. Her attention span was short, she was unable to make decisions, and sexual confusion was evident. She functioned best in a structured situation but functioned at a pre-school level. She was unable to write, had a low frustration tolerance, short attention span, and at times stared into space. She responded to structure in the school situation.

O. T. PLAN AND GOALS

Initial evaluation: Laura demonstrated inadequate visual motor skills and coordination on initial evaluation in O.T. She was cooperative but exhibited many facial grimaces and repeatedly jerked her head to the right, clicking her teeth. She seemed quite unsure of herself, had difficulty following verbal directions, and was disorganized in her approach to activities. She was easily distracted by and became preoccupied with minute, in-

significant stimuli such as the watermark on a sheet of
bond paper. She would begin tracing this, rather than
make the reproductions as instructed. She achieved
scores of 3 in skills, 5 in behavior, and 5 in relatedness.
Due to the degree of disorganization and distractibility
present, Laura was scheduled for individual sessions to
attempt to: establish a relationship, further observe her
behavior and skills, and to provide activities commensurate with her ability level.

Further observation in O.T. confirmed the extent of
Laura's disorganization and defective level of her skills
as seen initially. It became apparent she was functioning
at approximately a four-year old level. She liked to play
with dolls and seemed interested in sorting out reality
from fantasy. The grimacing and preoccupation with
minute stimuli persisted. The extent to which she could
form a meaningful relationship seemed minimal.

Continuing goals and plan: After a brief period of individual work aimed primarily at further evaluation,
Laura was placed in the basic skills group. The goals
were:

1. Provide structure, limit-setting, consistency and routine for patterning behavior.
2. Provide activities commensurate with her ability
level.
3. Provide reality orientation with clarification around
reality and fantasy.

Case 4. Darryl C., a nine-year old.

Description of the child: Darryl was referred to the
clinic because of a habit disorder (encopresis). He was
the fifth of ten children, ranging in age from four to
seventeen. Information concerning the family revealed
that the mother's ability to adequately fulfill this child's

44

dependency needs was questionable. The father was described as easy going, frequently unemployed, and frequently separated from the family.

CLINICAL FINDINGS

On psychological testing Darryl achieved a low average I.Q., full scale score 91, with a performance score of 93 and a verbal score of 90, with demonstrated deficits in perceptual motor skills. Perceptual scores on the Frostig Test of Visual Perception ranged from 5.9 to 6.9 with only one age-adequate score. Emotionally, Darryl was seen to be struggling with unresolved Oedipal rivalry and as having neurotic problems in the area of expression of anger and hostility. Unconscious destructive impulses were evident. He was described as being anxious to please, easily embarrassed by failure, and more comfortable with structure. The potential for acting-out aggressively in adolescence was noted. Neurological examination and EEG findings were within normal limits. The psychiatric formulations resulted in two diagnostic possibilities: passive-aggressive personality, or borderline character disorder with neurotic obsessive-compulsive features. Darryl was described by the psychiatrist as overly polite and friendly. He had a tendency to cling to him and was quite competitive with peers for his attention. He demonstrated immature superego formation and used isolation and overcompliance as defenses against anxiety. The potential for reality breakdown and regression under stress was seen as imminent. Unmet dependency needs, soiling, academic retardation, and perceptual difficulties were recognized as needing particular attention. The recommendations were:

1. Provide patterning experiences.

2. Provide perceptual retraining.
3. Provide habit training.
4. Develop superego.
5. Encourage male identification.
6. Encourage appropriate expression of anger.

Observations from the milieu: In the ward Darryl was described as pleasant, active, aggressive, and easily stimulated by his peers. His soiling continued during the day and he was enuretic at night. His gross motor coordination was described as adequate. His dependency needs appeared to be great.

In school he was functioning one year below expectancy in all academic areas. His reading skills were very poor with particular difficulty in ability to follow verbal directions. He was described as well-motivated but easily distracted by peers.

O.T. EVALUATION AND PLAN

Initial evaluation: Darryl demonstrated poorly developed visual motor skills, coordination, and non-verbal integration on initial evaluation in O.T. He related easily to the O.T. and demonstrated an adequate attention span and frustration tolerance. He scored 12 in skills, 11 in behavior, and 7 in relatedness. He was placed in the basic skills group for: further observation and evaluation, to establish a relationship, and to increase visual motor, coordination, and integration skills.

Further observation revealed that Darryl seemed deprived of simple investigatory experiences. His response to the activities in the group was delight. He needed direction and support in learning new activities, and sought praise, approval, and reassurance from the O.T.; he related easily and spontaneously but was easily distracted by peers and demonstrated a dislike for noise. He became resistive to the limits of the areas and began to tease and provoke peers.

Continuing plan and goals: The psychiatric recommendations as well as other related information were utilized in formulating the continuing plan for Darryl. The goals were:

1. Provide patterning experiences through limit setting, structure, and education in social interaction.
2. Maintain appropriate limits around behavior, pointing out and encouraging appropriate expression of anger in group situations.
3. Provide appropriate dependency gratification.
4. Point out reality around provocative behavior with peers.
5. Provide perceptual-motor retraining.

The previously formulated goals to increase visual motor, coordination, and integration skills in group activities were retained.

Darryl's progress during hospitalization was reviewed periodically. Improvement in both skills and behavior in O.T. resulted in his being moved into the intermediate group. His progress in school was described as slow. Handwriting was reported as improved. He continued to be distractible and appeared angry at the world.

In psychotherapy his behavior reactions were clarified, interpreted, and worked through. Ultimately he demonstrated less reliance on obsessive-compulsive defenses and reaction formation, but soiling continued. His final diagnosis was psychosis in remission, passive-aggressive personality with habit disturbance.

Case 5. Shirley L., an eleven-year old.

Description of the child: Shirley was referred to the clinic because of disruptive school behavior and inability to get along with peers.

Social history: Shirley's mother, forty-five, was described as somewhat confused and emotionally uninvolved with Shirley's problems. She blamed the child for all domestic problems, and was admittedly sexually promiscuous. Shirley's father had a long history of mental illness and was also promiscuous. Shirley was the second of four children. Her mother was reportedly disappointed that she had not been a boy.

CLINICAL FINDINGS

On psychological testing Shirley achieved a full scale I.Q. of 88, with a performance score of 85 and verbal score of 92. She was described as shy and quite concerned regarding failure. She saw human interaction as dangerous and ungratifying. She was seen to have characterological problems with psychotic tendencies and neurotic trends. Severe depression was evident. The psychiatric formulation resulted in a diagnosis of passive-aggressive personality disorder with regressive tendency. Shirley was described as aloof and attractive, a child whose major defenses were projection and regression. She was seen to be in need of consistency, patterning, and structure.

Observations from the milieu: In the ward Shirley was described as initially cheerful, euphoric, and restless; gradually becoming depressed, wandering aimlessly and becoming upset when routines changed. She evidenced masculine identification. She was described as competitive and having adequate coordination.

In school Shirley was described as generally cooperative with fluctuations in behavior from easily motivated, interested, and well-controlled to negative, resistive, and uncontrolled. She was described as lacking self-confidence.

O.T. Evaluation and Plan

Initial evaluation: Shirley related shyly with the O.T. and appeared to lack self-confidence. She worked slowly, was fairly well organized in her approach to the tasks, was attentive, and appeared to have adequate frustration tolerance. Her fine motor control and coordination were adequate. She achieved a score of 17 in skills, 9 in behavior, and 5 in relatedness. She was placed in the intermediate group with the goals: to reduce stress, establish a relationship, maintain adequate level of skills, and provide opportunities for successful accomplishments to raise her self-esteem.

Further observation revealed inadequate performance in a group. Shirley needed considerable support from the O.T., demonstrated low frustration tolerance, and was manipulative and demanding. She was slow in learning new processes and would have frequent temper outbursts during the learning stages. Once the activity or skill was learned, she worked quietly and well.

Continuing plan and goals: Based on the psychiatric formulation and other related information, the O.T. plan for Shirley included:

1. Support for feminine identification.

2. Opportunities for positive relationships with peers and adults.

3. Increase of frustration tolerance through success experiences. The initial goals to maintain adequate level of skills and provide opportunities for successful accomplishments were retained.

As Shirley's frustration tolerance, relationships with peers, and self-esteem improved she was moved into the advanced group. The goals were to support improved functioning and encourage appropriate social interaction and independence.

Case 6. John S., an eight-year old.

Description of child: John was referred to the clinic because of a habit disorder (encopresis) and reported hallucinations.

Social history: He was the youngest of two boys from an inadequate family. His mother, fifty-two, was totally deaf and blind. She was described as depressed, unable to communicate with others, and unable to care properly for John. John's father, fifty-three, was an alcoholic who was described as inconsistent in his handling of the boy and paranoid in his relationships. John's brother was convicted and imprisoned for armed robbery.

CLINICAL FINDINGS

Psychological testing revealed that John was of superior intelligence with a full scale I.Q. 122, performance I.Q. 107, and verbal I.Q. 132. He was described as anxious and depressed with strong feelings of hopelessness. His anxiety stemmed from unmet dependency needs. There was evidence of an ongoing schizophrenic process. His major defense against anxiety was intellectualization. It was recommended that therapy be aimed toward sealing over the psychotic process. The neurological evaluation was negative. The psychiatric formulation resulted in a diagnosis of passive-aggressive personality with psychotic episodes. John was seen as a child who had been raised by a mother unable to adequately gratify his dependency needs. He was isolated, rejected, and left to himself without structure or limits. His relationship with his father was inconsistent and his emotional life was in turmoil. His soiling was apparently his only avenue for the expression of anger. He was well defended, however, and could function adequately in structured situations but tended to become psychotic in situations that lacked structure.

Observations from the milieu: In the ward John was described as positively responsive to adults but aggressive toward peers. His soiling was evident. His skills in table games were poor to fair, and his conversation was dominated by fantasy.

In school John was functioning above chronological age expectancy, however he was unenthusiastic and too poorly motivated to perform academically.

O.T. EVALUATION AND PLAN

Initial evaluation: John demonstrated adequate visual motor skills and coordination on initial evaluation but had difficulty integrating parts into a meaningful whole. He followed directions well; his attention span and frustration tolerance were adequate. He appeared sad and was unspontaneous; however, he responded positively to praise. His scores were: skills 17, behavior 10, and relatedness 5. He was placed in the intermediate group with the goals of: establishing a relationship, and maintaining the level of his skills.

Further observation revealed that John frequently soiled in O.T. when he was angry. His frustration tolerance in the group was low and he would act out in response to disappointment or failure.

Continuing plan and goals: On the basis of this information, it became apparent that John needed to find more appropriate means of expressing his anger, to be provided with structure and limit-setting, and positive interpersonal relationships. The O.T. plan for John was to:

1. Maintain appropriate level of skills through participation in creative and constructive activities.
2. Provide structure, consistency, and predictability.
3. Encourage peer interaction in activities.
4. Encourage appropriate relationships with friendly adult females.
5. Encourage expression of anger in appropriate situations.

As John began to respond to treatment, he began projecting some of his anger and expressing it in art productions in the O.T. group. Because his associations to the productions were being lost during the time he was producing the objects, and due to the amount of stimulation both the work itself and the final products provided for the group, he was scheduled for individual sessions in O.T. to work through some of his anger using projective media.

Case 7. Irwin C., a five and one-half-year old.

Descriptions of the child: Irwin was referred to Lafayette because of depressive symptoms and withdrawal.

Social history: His father was described as sociopathic with passive-aggressive trends. He was unable to tolerate Irwin and expected the child to care for himself. Irwin's mother committed suicide when he was one and a half years old. Irwin's stepmother was described as immature and quite dependent. Irwin was one of three children.

CLINICAL FINDINGS

Psychological testing revealed uneven personality development with residues of difficulty from both oral and anal levels of development. He showed tendencies toward disorganization under stress. He achieved an I.Q.

of 100 which placed him in the average intelligence range. His perceptual-motor functioning was advanced. The neurological examination was negative. The EEG findings were within normal limits during sleep. The psychiatric formulation resulted in a diagnosis of adjustment reaction of childhood with neurotic trends. His restlessness and impulsivity were seen as manifestations of anxiety. He was seen to have a maturational lag along the psychosexual continuum.

Observations from the milieu: In the ward Irwin had difficulty relating with the children initially, and was quite dependent and overly affectionate with the staff. He had difficulty accepting limits.

In school he functioned at a readiness level in school activities. He was alert and followed directions well. His frustration tolerance was low but he responded well to re-direction and help from the teacher. He adjusted well to routine and classroom expectations.

O.T. EVALUATION AND PLAN

Initial evaluation: Irwin demonstrated transitional to adequate visual motor skills and coordination on initial evaluation in O.T. He related to the O.T. in a friendly, responsive, somewhat dependent manner. He was very alert and asked many questions. His attention span was short for each task and he appeared preoccupied at times. His scores were: skills 8, behavior 9, and relatedness 7. Irwin was placed in the basic skills group with the goals of: establishing a relationship, observing his behavior further, and providing appropriate activities.

Further observations revealed that he was able to work independently but demanded a great deal of attention and help. His skills as seen on initial evaluation remained transitional to adequate. He related in a dependent, affectionate but manipulative manner with the O.T. and had difficulty interacting with his peers.

Continuing plan and goals: Using the information from other sources and continued observations in O.T., the goals for Irwin were to:

1. Continue with the original plan.
2. Provide appropriate gratification of dependency needs.

Case 8. Marvin S., a ten-year old.

Description of the child: Marvin was referred to the clinic because of maladaptive behavior. He was described as shy, sensitive, and withdrawn. He had difficulty with peers, was a chronic complainer, and disliked doing his school work.

Social history: Marvin's mother, thirty-eight, was described as cooperative, responsive, and accepting of Marvin's need for psychiatric help. She was described as generally warm, stable, and mature; however, she was somewhat insecure in her role as a mother. She accepted the fact, however, that Marvin seemed to need more attention from her than the other children. There were four boys and one girl in this family. Marvin's father, thirty-nine, was described as athletic and extremely conscious of the difference between male and female roles.

CLINICAL FINDINGS

On psychological testing Marvin achieved a full scale I.Q. of 85, verbal I.Q. of 79, and a performance I.Q. of 99. The emotional difficulties that he experienced appeared to be secondary to cognitive-perceptual-motor dysfunction. He demonstrated difficulty in concept formation; thinking was concrete and his perceptual-motor skills were poor. He had underlying feelings of inadequacy and tended to become confused under stress. He showed evidence of unresolved Oedipal feelings, denied sexuality, and evidenced the potentiality for acting-out under stress. The neurological findings were positive in the motor areas. EEG findings were within normal limits. The psychiatric formulation resulted in a diagnosis of passive-dependent personality with academic deficits. Marvin was seen as a shy, unspontaneous, defensive child; aloof, detached, and whose affect was blunted. He appeared quiet, preoccupied, suspicious, and was a severe nail biter. His perceptual deficiencies were seen to be contributing to his feelings of inadequacy and his inability to function in social and academic situations. The recommendations for treatment were: raise self-esteem, improve self-image, develop age-appropriate defenses, increase affectual responses, provide masculine identification, and provide cognitive-perceptual-motor retraining. Social service contacts were to involve both parents; psychotherapy would be supportive and seek to clarify and interpret feelings and changes in performance and behavior as they occurred.

Observations from the milieu: In the ward Marvin was described as shy and affectually blunted. He sought affection and cuddling from the male staff members in an immature way. He tried very hard to compete favorably in physically active games but his skills were poor. He had difficulty relating with peers.

In the clinic school Marvin was functioning nine months below his chronological age grade placement, but in his previous school he had received fair to failing grades and had to be retained in kindergarten and third grade.

He performed well in the mechanical aspects of reading but had difficulty with comprehension and remembering. He had difficulty following verbal directions and his motor coordination was poor. His attitude toward school was indifferent with little motivation shown, and the need for constant direction to avoid confusion was evident. He expressed his feelings of inadequacy in school and was very dependent on the teacher.

O.T. Evaluation and Plan

Initial evaluation: Marvin demonstrated inadequate to transitional visual motor skills and coordination on the initial evaluation in O.T. He was quiet, somewhat withdrawn, and inhibited. He was cooperative but unspontaneous, responding only when questioned. He appeared somewhat confused initially, but was able to attend well to the tasks presented. His scores were: 13 in skills, 9 in behavior, and 4 in relatedness. He was placed in the basic skills group with the goals of: establishing a relationship, and further observation of his skills and behavior under reduced stress.

Further observation of Marvin confirmed the extent of the inadequacy of his skills. He continued to lack spontaneity and reacted to frustration by giving up. His interest in activities could be stimulated if the activities were within his capabilities and he could be allowed repetitive practice. Behaviorally, he was constricted and overly compliant to limit-setting.

Continuing plan and goals: On the basis of this information and recommendations, the O.T. goals for Marvin were revised to include:

1. Encourage expression of appropriate affect such as in situations evoking frustration, anger, and pleasure.
2. Teach social skills and appropriate ways of relating with others.

3. Provide perceptual-motor retraining.
The initial plan called for increase of visual motor skills and coordination. Activities for this were provided in the basic skills group while intensive perceptual-motor retraining was scheduled on an individual basis. When Marvin's skills and ability to relate improved, he was placed in the intermediate group.

Discussion of Cases

As seen from the cases presented, the use of a graded activity program does not preclude the use of other forms of therapy in the treatment of emotionally disturbed children, but rather allows for more systematic application of corrective experiences the child may benefit from. The individual personality dynamics, psychological and social needs, level of academic achievement, as well as the level of perceptual and motor development of the child, must be considered in our concern for helping the child develop adequacy and increasing the strength of his adaptive capacities. Patterning of behavior may be a primary need with some disturbed children and may need to be accomplished before the child can consistently benefit from skill development programs, academic programs, or formal psychotherapy—as in the case of Laura L. Other children may demonstrate a need for intensive perceptual-motor training beginning at an early developmental level—as in the case of Darryl C. Lack of achievement in these early areas may interfere with the adequate fulfillment of psychological needs necessary to the child's emotional growth and therefore retard the achievement of overall treatment objectives. Some children may demonstrate the need for working through conflicts in the psychological area. This need may represent a primary problem for some children, a secondary problem for others. In the case of John S., the need to express and work through his angry feelings was primary as it was seen to be interfering with his ability to benefit from other aspects of treatment, particularly his ability to relate to others; therefore it was necessary to direct specific attention to this particular problem during the course of his therapy.

4 Activity Group Programs

In a combined treatment-rehabilitation approach in occupational therapy, the activity groups constitute the core program and are supplemented by therapy on an individual basis with children who have specific problems in areas of psychodynamic conflict, and by training in individual or small group sessions for children who have gross defects in perceptual-motor functioning. The activities and relationships available to the children in the activity groups are designed to modify disordered concepts they have developed of themselves and the world.

BASIC SKILLS GROUP ACTIVITIES

The basic skills group is designed for children ranging in chronological age from six to twelve years who are functioning at a level of seven or below in their physical skills, are unpatterned or inadequately patterned in behavior, and who have difficulty relating to others at a level commensurate with their ages. The activities as well as the structure and orientation of the program for this group are designed to help the child develop or maintain adequate physical skills, achieve adaptive behavioral functioning, and develop skills in social interaction, which will result in improved feelings of adequacy and self-confidence and allow more positive interpersonal relationships. The program for this group includes a developmental play activity group and a skill development group.

The child who previously has had few experiences that would assist him in patterning his behavior and few opportunities for constructive, stimulating play experiences can achieve success and begin to view himself differently in an atmosphere that reduces stress initially, then encourages re-adaptation and re-learning along more acceptable lines. To reduce stress and provide corrective experiences for children, it is necessary to provide activities and relationships at the level of the child's capabilities through which he can learn by exploration, practice, and viewing his own progress.

In planning the developmental play phase of this group's program, the concept of the "prepared environment" has been used. The prepared environment is designed by an adult in advance of the child's entry into it. It is the physical and psychological situation made ready for the young child to enhance his opportunity to learn through experiences provided him. The "prepared environment is designed to help the child achieve a sense of himself, self mastery, and mastery of his environment through the successful execution and repetition of apparently simple tasks which are linked to the cultural expectations the child faces." *

* Nancy M. Rambusch, *Learning How to Learn: An American Approach to Montessori* (Baltimore, 1962), pp. 71–72.

For the emotionally disturbed child to make maximum use of such an experience, however, he may need directive help in the initial acquisition of fundamental skills. Many children with inadequately developed motor skills will successfully avoid those tasks and situations where they have encountered, or anticipate encountering, failure. To alter this behavior pattern, the skills development activity group is used to assist the child in acquiring adequate visual-motor and manipulative skills. Proficiency in the skill area enables the child to obtain success feedback in the environment of the play group and to give up the tendency to avoid such situations. The activities used to aid the child in the development of motor skills include: simple papercrafts, worksheets, clay modeling, and painting and drawing.

Because of the young child's need for consistency, the week is structured to promote a sense of security and contribute to independent functioning. As the child develops awareness of his schedule of activities he seems less confused in what is expected of him. Reminders are often necessary but are given in such a way as to reinforce the child's efforts to think about and remember his own schedule.

For instance, some children continually ask, "What do we do today?" The occupational therapist will ask, "What do we usually do on Thursday?" thus the child obtains the help he needs but has the opportunity to learn how to figure this out for himself. Changes in scheduling are announced in advance whenever possible to alleviate as much frustration as possible; however, spur-of-the-moment changes do occur and the children are helped to deal with these on the basis of reality factors and are given the support needed to accept the changes.

Figure 1 presents a sample weekly plan for this group.

It should be kept in mind that this is based on two hours per day that are not consecutive.

	Monday	Tuesday	Wednesday	Thursday	Friday
1st hour	playtime	playtime	playtime	painting	playtime
2nd hour	papercrafts	papercrafts	worksheets	worksheets	drawing
		coloring	coloring	coloring	clay modeling

Figure 1. Sample Weekly Schedule for Basic Skills Group

Play Activity Group

The play activity group is structured only in that the children are expected to play constructively with the toys, to take out what they wish to play with, and to return it to the toy cupboard when it is time to clean up.

On the first visit, the child is shown around the O.T. area and the location of toys and materials is pointed out so that he has some idea of what is available to him. When a child chooses a toy unfamiliar to him, he is instructed in at least one correct way of playing with it. The O.T. is careful not to infer that this is the only correct way but to allow the child the freedom of discovery. Pointing out one correct way gives the child the opportunity for immediate success and may then motivate him to try again. Having available only those play materials of particular benefit to the children and which they may freely handle eliminates the necessity for constant, nagging supervision.

The play area is equipped with such materials as:

picture books
regular building blocks
miniature town building blocks
supplies for play store
supplies for kitchen play (dishes, pans, refrigerator, and
    stove)
hammer and nail sets
pounding toys
graded picture puzzles

trucks, cars, airplanes
modeling clay
sound toys
record player and records
paints, paper and large brushes
crayons
fingerpaints
toys for water play
story books
take-apart toys
weighted cylinders
texture box
odors kit
dolls
design cubes
mosaic blocks
peg boards
paper dolls

A portion of one play period per week is used for directed, cooperative play in circle games such as Hokey Pokey and Looby Loo. As a matter of course the children are free to play individually or cooperatively as they choose.

Many of the children who have been placed in this group begin at the level of solitary, exploratory play and progress to the level of cooperative play demonstrating an increase in the ability to share and take turns. The use of circle games enhances growth in this direction and offers an opportunity for the therapist to gauge progress as it occurs.

Skill Development Group

The skill development activity group is structured in expectation as well as in activities. The children are made aware that this time is set aside for these activities and that they are expected to participate. The activities are chosen by the O.T. with choices of color and arrangement in their individual project left up to the child. The activities presented to the children have been graded in complexity and have been selected to develop or increase fine motor control, eye-hand coordination, and visual perception skills. Cut paper activities are graded from tracing geometric forms using stencils (which provide the child with external control), through tracing animal forms using patterns (which are more complex and require more control from the child) (see Figure 2). Different colors and textures of paper may be used. The children may cut out the figures that are traced.

Figure 2. Sample Patterns for Visual Motor Activities

These may be pasted on larger paper and scrapbooks may be made of them. Color, form, and texture are discussed and emphasized in this activity.

The children are allowed as much time as necessary to complete each project. The emphasis is placed on doing the activity, enjoying the doing, and not on the finished product. Mastery of the skills involved is felt to be more important than the colors chosen or placement of forms at this point in our program.

Worksheets used to develop skills in this area include standard educational reading readiness worksheets, Frostig Visual Perception Worksheets, and others. Coloring books, coloring book pictures, and other activity book projects such as dot-to-dot pictures with numbers are also used, specifically to increase visual motor skill and perception.

Painting in this program is a free expression and developmentally oriented experience. Those children who have difficulty with such a free activity on the basis of psychological dynamic factors are nevertheless encouraged to paint for a part of the hour then allowed to do other things. The time is increased as much as possible over a long period of time until the child is able to accept the activity and enjoy it. This session is planned specifically to allow the child to develop and experience free expression at his current level of development. As he masters the skills associated with that level, he can be seen moving on to the next level and is given the emotional support needed.

Clay modeling and drawing are activities directed initially. The fundamentals of drawing, based on the use of geometric shapes, are satisfying, especially to children who have had minimal success in drawing previously. In clay modeling, discussion about objects which can be made, those we see daily, those we use, those which we know about but do not see can be used for stimulation. In these sessions verbal questioning is used to elicit the children's own ideas and to help them think through problem areas. When making animals, for instance, it is possible to talk about animals they have seen, trips to the zoo, pets they have at home, and their favorite animals. Demonstration is used most effectively and the children's responses as to where the head, legs, and tail should be placed are discussed during the demonstration process.

In the skills activity group the children sit around a large table. Instructions for each new activity are presented to the group as a whole, followed up by individual attention and help as needed. As the children in this group who are above seven years experience mastery of the skills, adjustment in behavior, and relationships associated with this level, they may be moved into the intermediate group; however, the children who are appropriately placed according to age remain and continue to reinforce the learning which has taken place.

INTERMEDIATE GROUP ACTIVITIES

The intermediate group is designed for children whose skills and behavior functioning fall generally into the eight to nine year range but who may be actually eight to twelve years old. At this level there continues to be a need for practice in physical skills while the need for developing organizational ability, independence of functioning, and positive group interaction become more important. Children who are ten or older and who need to develop adequacy in any of these functional areas may be placed in this group. The activities for this group are designed to bridge the gap between the simple tasks performed by the children at the level of those in the basic skills group and the more complex activities required of the advanced group. The emphasis is placed on developing and utilizing the visual motor and perception skills required for executing projects requiring organization, ability to follow complex verbal instructions, increased work tolerance, and attention. A gradual increase in independence is fostered and emphasis on group interaction is gradually increased.

Some of the projects utilized in this group include:

papier mâché masks
paper bag masks
paper sculpture decorations
drawing from experience
coloring
painting (using experimental approach)
crayon overlay
jigsaw puzzles
boy and girl put-together figures
airplanes, cars, trucks, boats (using cardboard and paper)
totem poles

gadget printing
stained glass windows
holiday greeting cards
mobiles
kites
puppets
paper mat weaving
worksheets (to develop visual motor skills and coordination)
murals (depicting underwater life and frontier life)
zoos (including the construction of cages and three-dimensional animals)

A directive approach is also used in presenting the activities for this group. Group instructions are given and are followed up by individual help as needed. The children are expected to participate in all activities presented. As the children gain proficiency, less help from the therapist is needed and they are in a position to assist peers and work together constructively with them.

The concept of a "free day" is used with this group to develop constructive use of free time and provide an opportunity to gauge the children's readiness and capacity for independence. Free day occurs once every two weeks and may be used as the child wishes; however, he is required to use the time constructively. Children who are initially unable to organize themselves and their time well enough to work productively and efficiently are not pressured. They are given enough time to choose a direction but not allowed to reach the point of becoming unbearably frustrated. The therapist will make suggestions to guide the child in structuring a task for himself which may include ideas and techniques he has previously learned in the regular group sessions.

Cooperative projects are particularly encouraged in this group. Initially, it is necessary for the therapist as group leader to help the group in its decision-making regarding the project to be made; however, as the children develop in their skills, relationships, and self-confidence they take over much of the decision-making and are able to carry out a cooperative project with minimal assistance from the occupational therapist. Bulletin boards and murals are examples of successful cooperative projects for this age group.

As the children in this group who are chronologically ten or older progress in skills, ability to function cooperatively, and capacity for independent functioning they may be moved into the advanced group. Those children who have been appropriately placed in this group according to age remain and continue to reinforce the learning that has taken place.

Advanced Group Activities

The advanced group is designed for children who have obtained mastery of the basic physical skills and have the capacity to function in a constructive, independent manner both in activities and social situations. This group requires the most from the child in terms of independent functioning and is planned to provide instruction in various crafts and activities of interest to the pre-adolescent. As with the other two groups, the children are expected to participate in all activities. The activities for this group are presented in units, that is, several processes all involving the use of one material or technique are presented in sequence, allowing the child to learn each of these techniques and providing additional opportunity for the child to work independently and make use of the knowledge he has gained.

As each new unit is introduced, the occupational therapist talks with the children about the media to be used, explaining the processes and the possible uses for the products to be made (whether utilitarian, decorative, simply for the experience, or for fun). Samples are used to give the children an idea of what the finished project will be. (We have found that words are not enough.) Each new activity is explained or demonstrated, giving step-by-step instructions. Any relationships that exist between the new activity and a previous one, relative to techniques learned, is pointed out.

The children are asked to keep all projects made during each unit in their shelves in the O.T. area until the unit is completed. After the unit is completed the finished pieces are brought into the group, reviewed, and discussed. The children are almost always amazed at how much they have accomplished and how well they have done. We feel that some of this feeling of accomplishment is lost if the child takes each finished project with him as it is completed.

The following activity units may be presented in any order that seems most logical for the group it will be used for. The sequence within the units has been worked out, tested, changed, and has proven successful in this order:

mosaic techniques:
    fundamentals of design specific to mosaics
    paper mosaic projects (pictures)
    mosaic tile projects (boxes and trivets)
    vegetable and seed projects (pictures)
    gravel mosaic projects (pictures)
    collage projects (pictures and boxes)
    select final project from this series.
leather crafts:
    keycase or coin purse
    wallet
    mocassins
    select final project from this series.
metal crafts:
    fundamentals of design specific to metalwork
    project using metal tapping (wall hanging and trivet)

metal tooling project (picture)
metal etching (trays and coasters)
metal forming (bowls and trays)
metal enameling (jewelry, bowls, and trays)
select one process for final project.
decorative printing techniques:
fundamentals of design specific to printing
vegetable printing (carrots and potatoes)
linoleum block printing (on paper and cloth)
stenciling
silk screen process
select one process for final project.
ceramics and sculpture:
ceramics
pinch method
slab method
coil method
free form method
sculpture with clay
select one process for final project.
creative arts techniques:
sketching
objects (spheres, boxes, cylinders and tools)
still life (flower arrangements and fruit)
animals
people (sitting, in motion, and in groups)
scenes around the hospital or away from the hospital.
chalk drawing
watercolor
oil painting
experimental techniques
crayon rubbings
sandpaper drawings
dribble painting (lacquer on white masonite)
yarn painting
rubber cement resist
tempera on wet paper
select final activity from all techniques learned.

The mosaic techniques unit presents a unique opportunity for experiences in recognizing similarities and differences in texture and design, as the techniques and materials involved in making paper and tile mosaics are similar, while those involved in vegetable and gravel mosaics are similar. Some of both techniques may be utilized in college. Instructions in the fundamentals of design for mosaics is helpful in developing recognition of the possibilities as well as the limitations of this medium.

Kits are utilized exclusively in the leather crafts unit. Reality factors and the possibility of the carryover value for a hobby were considered in making this choice. It was considered that groups of normal children of this age (Boy Scouts, Girl Scouts, and Indian Guides) often use kits rather than hides in their experiences with leather, and that if a child developed an interest in this activity for use as a hobby, the information gained in learning to begin his own project, following written directions or diagrams, and finishing his own project would be of value. The three items chosen offer a continuum of increasing complexity of the techniques used, the organizational and integration ability needed, and the necessity for following directions.

In the metal crafts unit the children are encouraged to create original designs and are instructed in the fundamentals of design for metalwork. This unit provides excellent experience with texture and dimensions.

The decorative printing techniques unit is graded in complexity of technique and the processes involved. The fundamentals of design specific to printing are particularly important in the aspects of negative and positive images and concepts of foreground and background.

In ceramics and sculpture the children are exposed to several clay modeling techniques, instructed in the properties and uses of glaze, and in the terminology associated with this activity. Seeley Thompson's *Activities in Cera-*

71

mics (Bloomington, Ill., 1956) has been quite useful for this unit.

In the creative arts techniques unit discussion and demonstration are used initially. Light, shadow, color, texture, and technique are discussed. Sketching is presented first in the unit and the sketches and ideas developed in this section may be used in chalk drawing, watercolor, and oil painting. The experimental techniques yield particularly satisfying results for many of the children and do require some judgment, sense of responsibility, and motivation. The extent to which this unit is used is dependent only on the knowledge and skill of the therapist. The *My World of Art Series* (Chicago), and Mary Blac Diller's *Drawing for Young Artists* (New York, 1955) have been most useful for this unit.

The children are expected to choose a final project in each unit to be carried out utilizing the techniques and processes learned in that unit. At this point in the unit it would be expected that the child could work independently, would be in control of the media, and could successfully accept this responsibility. This type of response can occur within each unit. As the children gain proficiency, they become less dependent on the therapist, are more likely to seek help if needed from a peer, and will spontaneously offer help to each other. At this point also the therapist is in the role of an available but inactive leader of the group.

APPLICATION OF THIS CONCEPT

Due to the nature of the administrative policies and the function of Lafayette Clinic, the child population is subject to fairly rapid turnover. The maximum length of stay possible for any given child is two years; the minimum is approximately six weeks.

Although the activity program described here has been developed in such a setting, it has application for other settings where the turnover is less frequent and children are hospitalized for longer periods. Within the scope of each activity group there is considerable opportunity to broaden the program yet remaining within the developmental framework of that level. For instance, in the basic skills group the number of play materials which could be utilized is limitless as well as the number of games, patterns, stencils and possibilities of working with paints and clay. Besides these possibilities the value of repetition and reinforcement using the same materials should not be overlooked. Most often those children who are in need of long-term hospital care are those who have the least effective adaptive skills and behavior and may need longer opportunity for success feedback to benefit sufficiently. It should be remembered, particularly with the basic skills group, that repetition which may appear boring to an adult is the child's way of learning.

With the intermediate group the projects which can be utilized within the framework of the objectives outlined for that group is limited only by the ingenuity and resourcefulness of the individual leading the group. The sources for these types of activities are many. The free day activities may be enhanced by the availability of usable discards such as shirt cardboards, empty boxes, and scrap paper of various kinds.

Each of the units within the advanced group could be expanded to include production of several projects using each of the learned techniques. For instance, in the metal crafts unit it may be possible and quite desirable to make several projects using each of the metal decorating and forming techniques. It would also be possible to extend the complexity upward when the unit was repeated to allow for continued growth and accomplishment. Other

73

activities may be introduced and graded, such as weaving which could include paper weaving, cardboard loom fingerweaving, weaving with raffia, and Indian bead weaving. Woodworking could be added to this group's activities in those settings where this is ordinarily a part of the occupational therapy sphere and an industrial arts program is not available.

It is important to maintain as much autonomy as possible, however, within each activity group regarding the activities used, as this provides a portion of the incentive which may be engendered and utilized to encourage the children and support their efforts to grow up. The children can be provided with tangible evidence of their progress and can rely on their own reality testing for some of the necessary feedback which contributes to feelings of adequacy, increased self-esteem, and self-confidence.

HANDLING MALADJUSTED BEHAVIOR

Within each group the behavior the children manifest that is disruptive to their own functioning as well as to the functioning of the group should be handled according to the needs of the individual and the expectations of behavior for that group. (The child's capacity for functioning at the level expected of him should be assessed at the time that the treatment plan is formulated since consultation with the psychotherapist may be necessary to determine this.) The effectiveness of various controls may be determined by trial and terror and reassessment of the situation. Any of the controls outlined in Chapter 2 may be attempted. The usual initial sequence for helping the child whose behavior is disruptive to the group's functioning is removal from the group to an area outside the O.T. workroom. (If there is enough space within the workroom but away from the group, it may be helpful to remove the child there first.) If the child can recover sufficiently within a reasonable time, he may be returned to the group. However, if he becomes more disruptive, it may be necessary to return him to the living unit. When a child must be removed from the group situation, the reasons for and circumstances around his removal should be explained to him as clearly as possible since many children interpret such behavior by adults as rejection and evidence of their being unloveable.

Situations may arise within the group where behavior takes place, such as swearing, which for some children may be tolerated to the point at which it becomes disruptive to the group's functioning. This type of behavior may be handled by ignoring it initially; however, if it must be controlled, the reasons for this should be stated so that the child becomes aware of the socially unacceptable qualities of the behavior which are distinct from his acceptability as an individual.

Other behavioral reactions may occur which are related to the personality dynamics of the child. In such a case the reasons for the disturbed behavior may not be readily discernible in the specific group situation. Handling this type of behavior requires knowledge of the child from a dynamic point of view so that the basis for his fears, insecurities, and imagined injustices can be understood and dealt with appropriately. For instance, the child who has previously had little experience with consistent adults who keep promises and are there when needed will have difficulty accepting this state of affairs as a natural part of living and may be unable to tolerate being promised that his project will be in his shelf the next day when he returns to the O.T. area. Inappropriate behavior accompanying the difficulty in accepting such a promise may be handled by anticipating the child's feelings, verbalizing them, and empathizing with them but holding to the expectation and the promise. It is then extremely important to follow through making sure that the promise is kept. Only then can a sense of trust be initiated.

The technique of anticipating and verbalizing the child's feelings in a particular situation may be helpful also to children who displace their feelings, who are demanding in such a way as to inevitably incur rejection and non-gratification of their demands, as well as with children who are inhibited and have difficulty expressing affect appropriately and relating with others on a social level.

Reality orientation and clarification may be used with children who behave in a provocative, teasing manner with other children and who complain that nobody likes them or wants to play with them, as well as with the shy, withdrawn child who is fearful of personal interaction. Educational techniques using concrete suggestion and demonstration in more appropriate ways of relating with other children, as well as with adults, may also be helpful.

It is particularly important to be informed of changes in the child's clinical behavior in other areas of the milieu and in psychotherapy to intelligently judge whether the behavior he displays in the O.T. area is a situational reaction or a generalized one. It is important to be informed also of anticipated changes in the child's behavior due to medication or psychotherapy. Inappropriate behavior which is associated with the expression of affect in a child who has previously been unable to, for example, must be handled in certain situations relative to its appropriateness or inappropriateness. But it is helpful to the child under these circumstances if the adult can communicate his understanding of and pleasure in seeing the child achieve this level of adjustment. Knowledge of the psychotherapy goals for such a child will allow the O.T. to reinforce progress as it occurs.

INTEREST GROUPS

Supplementary to the activity groups designed to develop mastery of life skills may be groups designed to consolidate the gains made in the core activity program. Such groups may be formed around a mutual interest of the group such as music, cooking, drama, and gardening. The effectiveness of these groups will depend largely on the maturity and confidence that the children have developed and may be used as additional incentives in the growth process.

PHYSICAL FACILITIES

Some aspects of the physical facilities to be used in carrying out this type of program are worth consideration. The developmental play program for the basic skills group requires a play area equipped with tables, chairs, bookshelves, toy shelves, storage bins, miniature kitchen, and doll furniture. The other programs carried on in the activity groups require a work area also equipped with tables and chairs as well as storage cupboards for each child's work and for supplies and materials.

For the storage of toys sliding door cabinets with shelves have proven to be more satisfactory for use by the children than the traditional toy bin, regardless of its size. We have, however, found it difficult to eliminate the toy bin entirely as there seems to be a need for a catch-all in a play area. It cannot, however, be the major source of toy storage due to the disorganization which develops and contributes to the increased incidence of broken toys, and the inability to easily discern the nature of its contents. The consideration and acquisition of such small items in the play area as puzzle storage racks and transparent plastic containers for beads and blocks can greatly facilitate the child's ability to find play materials on his own and can reinforce his independence.

As to furniture, molded plywood stacking chairs and formica-topped tables of varying shapes have proven to be useful, flexible, and quite durable in our setting. The use of individual storage compartments for each child is useful in terms of organization of the workroom but more importantly can be used to further the assumption of responsibility and increase the feeling of belonging by the children. Storage cupboards for frequently used supplies should be located in the work area, easily accessible to both the children and staff.

Whether the play area and work area are combined may necessarily be determined by the availability of space. If the areas are combined, the time for each activity can be so determined as to avoid confusion. If a separate playroom is available, this room could be used for individual therapy as well. Enclosed areas have proven more satisfactory for this group than large, open areas. The children's activities can then be confined within a reasonable space and supervision can be more effective. A kitchen area equipped with range, refrigerator, sink, tables, chairs, counter, and cupboard space would be necessary for cooking activities. This area could be combined with the playroom or exist as a separate unit. An outdoor area suitable for planting would be necessary to carry out gardening activities.

STAFF

To carry out the entire program as discussed in this handbook, a minimum ratio of one full-time registered occupational therapist per twenty children is recommended. In our setting the children are seen in small groups of not more than eight children per group in the core program. With comprehensive scheduling in other areas such as school, R.T., and industrial arts, four hours of occupational therapy a day per O.T. is possible.

5 Individual Programs

Group activity programs are sufficient to meet many of the needs of disturbed children; however, individual sessions in occupational therapy may be indicated in addition to participation in group activities for those children who require intensive work designed even more specifically to develop appropriate means of identification and expression, appropriate behavior patterns, and re-training in perceptual-motor functions.

Intensive work requires close coordination with individual psychotherapy since the reaction patterns which are developed as a result of the participation in occupational therapy should be reinforced, supported by, and integrated with individual psychotherapy for maximum benefit.

Individual sessions may be scheduled from one-half to one full hour or more a day, from two to five times a week, depending on the nature of the problem and the time available for individual, intensive work. When intensive work is undertaken it is important to the child that the schedule of sessions is regular and consistent, and that the child is aware of what is expected of him as well as any limitations in the individual therapy situation that may be different from those encountered in the group. It is important to the child that the therapist is honest in his reactions, consistent in handling behavior, and totally reliable.

The factor that distinguishes individual intensive work from the group activity program is its concentration on one or two major problem areas and the 1:1 patient-therapist ratio. The individual program should be designed to attack, correct, or modify a specific component of behavior or skill and should terminate when the goal is reached.

Modification of Psychological Processes

Individual intensive work may be undertaken to develop more appropriate identification, masculine or feminine; to encourage free expression of feelings; to develop independent functioning; to encourage appropriate constructive expression of impulses; to increase feelings of self-worth; and to improve self-concept. As can be readily seen, these are goals that are not unique to individual work in O.T. but may be fostered in the group as well. Intensive work on a 1:1 basis will, however, permit more specific concentration on the primary problem of the individual child.

The choice of media should coincide with the nature of the goal to be reached. Activities to be used to increase feminine identification, for instance, should be selected with that goal in mind. It may be necessary to begin with neutral activities and grade them toward more feminine aspects.

Media which allow for projection of feeling and emotion should be used to encourage freedom of expression. The child may be presented with a choice: pencil and paper, poster paint or watercolor, clay or fingerpaint. The child will choose those media he feels most comfortable with and will become more expressive in his productions as ego growth takes place. For instance, the child who is extremely constricted and compulsive may choose pencil and paper as his media initially. As the sessions progress and as growth takes place, he will become less restricted, more comfortable and more expressive, and begin to use paint, clay, or fingerpaint.

The reverse may be true for the child who needs satisfaction of regressive impulses. He may choose fingerpainting and his work may be characteristic of that of a much younger child; however, as he progresses he will be able to give up his regressive smearing, gain control of his impulses, and begin to utilize clay, paints, and pencil and paper.

Children who need an outlet for appropriate expression of their impulses may also be encouraged to utilize projective media. The content of their productions may be more important than the choice of media. For instance, the child's productions may be initially bizarre and unrealistic; as he progresses more realism may be observed in his productions.

Occupational therapy aimed at psychodynamic problems and unconscious psychological processes should be goal-oriented, non-directive, and skillfully executed. The relationship of the O.T. to the child is important from the standpoints of acceptance, empathy, objectivity, and sensitivity. The relationship itself may or may not be the crucial variable depending on the goals to be reached but must have these four qualities as its basis.

A satisfactory working relationship must be developed between the occupational therapist and the child such that each respects the other's role. This relationship should be distinguished from the psychotherapeutic relationship used in individual psychotherapy, since the changes that take place within the child as a result of special techniques in O.T. derive as much from the specific media used as from the relationship with the therapist.

Our intention here is not to downgrade the value of the individual interpersonal relationship. However, careful observations have led us to believe that the positive aspects of the relationship with the occupational therapist derive as much from the success component of the child's experience as from the acceptance and understanding by the O.T. This is by no means a small contribution, but the child also participates in this experience and the success he derives from accomplishment, release, and mastery must also be considered as relating to the change that occurs. The emotional growth that takes place during the course of individual, intensive work appears to emerge spontaneously. The following examples serve to illustrate case-finding, goal-direction, and techniques.

Case Illustration 1

John S., age eight was recommended for individual therapy in O.T. during the fifth month of his hospitalization. He had been referred to the clinic because of a habit disorder (encopresis) and reported hallucinations. His plan of treatment included individual psychotherapy, pharmacotherapy, and milieu therapy.

By the fourth month of hospitalization, clinical findings revealed that he was of superior intelligence and was described as anxious and depressed. He showed evidence of an on-going schizophrenic process; intellectualization was his major defense against anxiety.

John was a child whose dependency needs had been

inadequately met as were his needs for structure and discipline. His soiling was viewed as his only apparent avenue for the expression of anger. He appeared well-defended and able to function adequately in structured situations, tending to become psychotic in situations that lacked structure.

Observations in O.T. revealed that John initially worked in an organized manner in activities, was quick to grasp new ideas, and carried out his work with good motivation, interest, and understanding. His visual motor skills and his attention span were adequate and he concentrated well. He gradually became more spontaneous and more verbal in his relationships with peers. His conversations were appropriate and reality-oriented.

During the third month of hospitalization, John began to show particular interest in free day and would use this time to make elaborate macabre projects such as haunted houses filled with skulls, snakes, rats, cobwebs, ghosts, skeletons, and witches. During this same period he was beginning to express some resentment and anger regarding the demands made of him in the O.T. area such as for cleaning up at the end of the hour. He began to react to frustration in his activities by attempting to avoid frustration or ignore it, and from his peers by yelling at them and threatening them with physical violence. He continued to do well on structured activities. His attention span and his skills remained adequate.

It was recommended that John begin individual therapy in O.T. to encourage constructive expression of his impulses. It was recognized that he had a tendency toward psychotic disorganization in unstructured situations. However, it was felt that his ego strength and defenses generally were strong enough to withstand the impact of this technique. The structure of the remainder of his program was supportive to ego integration.

Projective media were used. The choice included pencil and paper, painting, and clay modeling. He was seen twice a week for half-hour sessions over a four-month period. During the first session John chose pencil and paper and made a drawing of "a war scene between the Japanese and Americans. The Japanese had one tank, one missile and some ground troops. The Americans had two bombers, two tanks and ground forces. There was lots of bombing and killing." He verbalized freely as he was working. As he was drawing a B-48 Hustler, he explained that it could fly at twice the speed of sound.

His affect was essentially flat, however, and he denied having any feelings about anything. When asked how he felt about visiting groups coming through the area he said, "I don't know. I didn't notice them." Later, he smiled and talked spontaneously about a ward party and a relay race that his team had won, but he could not admit he was pleased about it.

John chose clay modeling during his second session continuing with aircraft and guns and explained that "the reason that I'm making everything gray is because everything in the army just about is made out of gray steel."

For the third session he chose painting. He talked about a television program he had seen the night before called *Rocket to the Moon*: "The moon was inhabited by all ladies and spiders. The men who went to the moon were afraid to take off their space suits because the women might hurt them. They didn't, though. They got friendly." He continued painting while he was talking. "The spider ripped the space man's suit off and the ladies burned up the spider." He talked about the ladies being weird. When asked whether they were scary or just funny-looking he replied that they were "sorta scary and sorta funny-looking. They wore their hair like this"—

drawing a picture of it. I remarked that it looked like the way I wear my hair. He said "yes, and they wore purple suits, had sharp points on their ears and pointed eyebrows." He went on to explain that "the lady in his painting was going after the blob so that it can't hurt the man. She already made the spider start burning up. She used heat rays. She just points her finger and the heat rays come out. The animals had powers such as death vision and stuff like that." We talked about the possibility of sharing his productions with his doctor at this point and made an agreement to do so after the next session. During the next session he chose clay modeling and made a "future museum."

John continued to register mood changes and changes in affect which he could not relate to the immediate source of pleasure, anger, or frustration. He continued to produce paintings, drawings, and clay modelings that were destructive and aggressive in subject matter.

Toward the end of the second month, he had a fight with one of his peers. He talked about how it started and how he had fared. His reply to "Did you enjoy the fight?" was "No!" When asked why, he said "because he got a foot lock on my head." During this session John drew a huge oven for baking pottery which he said was "like what the Indians used" (his regular O.T. group was doing ceramics and sculpture at this time). From this point on John's productions were more oriented toward events from everyday life at the clinic and at this point it was decided to encourage him to associate his feelings with the stimulus for them, pointing out reality to him and suggesting ways of dealing with it. John often appeared sleepy when he was angry. When questioned about his being angry or the source of his anger, the O.T. would point out the appropriateness of the response without giving license to uncontrolled retaliation. The same was true of pleasurable experiences. The opportunity was taken to explain how other people feel and behave in such situations.

During the fourth month of individual work, John had another fight with a peer. He explained what happened as he had previously and related that he had hit the child in retaliation. When asked about how he felt about it, he said "Good!" This was reinforced both in terms of appropriateness and reality. As John continued to progress, his associations to his productions continued to be more reality-centered. Many of the objects he made really looked very much like earlier productions but his associations were less destructive. For instance, one clay modeling of a man holding a huge "rock" above his head "broke the chains that held him and threw the rock down and killed all of the people." Toward the end of the sessions, an almost identical figure was a "deep-sea diver who was going down to the bottom of the sea for treasure."

Case Illustration 2

Amy S., a ten-year old, was scheduled for individual sessions in occupational therapy to encourage feminine identification. She was referred to the clinic due to hyperactive, destructive, and impulsive behavior. She proved to be quite dextrous and enjoyed making complicated toys, planting things. and caring for animals. Amy's I.Q. on the Wechsler Intelligence Scale was 110, which placed her in the bright-normal range. She was described as overly affectionate with her father and as having identified more with him than with her mother who would have preferred Amy to be a boy. Limits had not been placed on her behavior at home since the parents preferred to give in to her rather than have her become upset.

The structure of the hospital milieu, medication, and

psychotherapy aided Amy toward a better behavioral adjustment. Academically she was quite capable, her skills were adequate in games and activities, and her behavior became more acceptable. As a pre-teen it was felt that Amy could benefit from exposure to feminine activities and a positive relationship with a friendly, accepting adult female.

Amy was scheduled for two half-hour sessions a week for eight weeks. The activities chosen were feminine-oriented and included making a scrapbook, planting flower seeds, making paper flowers, jewelry, soap sachet, baking, sewing, knitting, and crocheting. Genuine enjoyment of frankly feminine pursuits and being a girl were the chief objectives of the program. Appropriate behavior for pre-teen girls was emphasized and rewarded by verbal approval.

To accomplish the goals set for Amy, it was necessary to support and reassure her in an area potentially very threatening and difficult. Initially, her mother did not appreciate her being a girl and although she did change somewhat Amy had to be helped to realize that she could be accepted as a girl by others. During the fifth week Amy reported she had shown her mother the net and soap sachet she had made but her mother didn't say anything about it. Amy's comment was, "I guess she just doesn't like fancy things," and she went ahead with her activities without becoming upset or discouraged. By the end of six weeks Amy's interest in wearing dresses had increased as well as her interest in wearing curls rather than a butcher boy haircut.

Development of Cognitive-Perceptual-Motor Functions

Children who manifest problems in behavior such as hyperactivity, autistic preoccupation, short attention span, distractibility, and withdrawal, who evidence academic difficulties in reading, writing, or arithmetic; and who evidence skill deficiencies such as inadequate coordination and motor control, may be found to have cognitive-perceptual-motor dysfunction which will respond favorably to intensive re-training in the areas of defect.

Individual work* in perceptual-motor re-training† involves intensive stimulation in areas of functional defect. The aim is to modify the primary dysfunction rather than to substitute compensatory modes of adaptation. Perceptual motor re-training may be distinguished from group activity by the intensity and specificity of its application. The assumption underlying this approach is that adequate cognitive-perceptual-motor skills will allow the child to function more successfully in academic and social areas, thus helping him develop a better concept of himself and increased self-esteem.

The re-training method consists of presenting the child with activities specifically selected to correct or modify a particular perceptual-motor dysfunction at the level at which he can achieve immediate success. The activities are then graded along a continuum of complexity from that point. The activities used in perceptual-motor re-training include sensory stimulation, physical exercise, academic readiness materials, play materials, educational toys, and specifically designed perceptual-motor training materials. The approach to the child is directive.

The perceptual-motor functions in which re-training

---

* Re-training may be accomplished with small groups of children providing the functions to be trained are similar and the experience of the therapist permits.

† In this handbook "cognitive-perceptual-motor," "cognitive-motor," and "perceptual-motor" are used interchangeably.

can most effectively be accomplished in occupational therapy are: tactile-proprioceptive perception; motor functions, including coordination of extremities, fine motor control, and eye-hand coordination; visual perception; spatial orientation; and non-verbal integration. Cognitive functions concerned with abstraction, conceptual thinking, remembering, and symbolic integration as well as other perceptual functions (such as audition and verbal expressiveness which may also be impaired in the disturbed child) may be more suitably trained by individuals who are specifically trained in special education or speech correction but may be included in any perceptual-motor re-training plan. Coordinated training programs that will provide comprehensive cognitive-perceptual-motor re-training for children as required may be accomplished through the cooperative effort of occupational therapists, special education teachers, recreational therapists, and others. (Working definitions of all of the cognitive-perceptual-motor functions, assessment techniques, and suggested training techniques developed by the Lafayette Clinic interdisciplinary research team* are in Appendix C.)

In our setting children who demonstrate gross inadequacies on the Occupational Therapy Evaluation Battery; who are two or more years retarded in any academic area; who manifest perceptual-motor deficits on psychological testing; and who demonstrate autistic preoccupation, hyperactivity, withdrawal, excessive distractibility, and short attention span would be considered for evaluation on the Cognitive-Perceptual-Motor Battery.

In each of the cognitive-perceptual-motor functions delineated, the child is evaluated and rated on a con-

---

* The Lafayette Clinic research team represents psychology, special education, occupational therapy, and recreational therapy.

tinuum of chronological age expectancy in which AD means advanced beyond age expectancy; AP, appropriately developed for age; SD, somewhat deficient; and MD, markedly deficient. Children who are found to be somewhat to markedly deficient in perceptual-motor functioning are considered for intensive re-training.

TRAINING PROCEDURE

In the initial stages of perceptual-motor re-training it is important to elicit the child's cooperation and attempt to evaluate the level of his motivation. These factors will influence the manner in which the child involves himself in his training. It is important also to explain to the child that the program he has been selected for has been planned specifically for him, delineating the areas in which the program is designed to correct (to help him learn to move more efficiently, write more smoothly, read more effectively, or get along better with others). Concrete examples of the child's difficulties in school performance or general behavior may be used to help the child understand the necessity for such a program.

The essential factors in the perceptual-motor re-training process are: the level at which it begins; the use of repetition and reinforcement; and careful grading of the activities presented. As mentioned earlier, the method of presenting the materials is initially adjusted to the child's level of successful achievement even though this level may fall in the six-month-to-one-year developmental range. It is then increased in complexity from that point. The concentration of materials is intensive and exposure time in a particular activity may be graded from unlimited to limited as the child gains proficiency. Two case examples are presented to illustrate the evaluation and training procedure:

Case Illustration 1

Douglas C., a nine-year old, was referred to the clinic because of encopresis. He was considered for cognitive-perceptual-motor evaluation because of demonstrated difficulties on the Occupational Therapy Evaluation; left-right confusion; and academic difficulty in reading, in ability to follow verbal directions, and in handwriting. His attention span was short and his frustration tolerance was low. He scored in the low average range on the Wechsler Intelligence Scale with disparate performance on individual sub-tests. He achieved 5.9 to 6.9 age scores on the Frostig Developmental Test of Visual Perception with only one age-appropriate score. On the Cognitive-Perceptual-Motor Battery, he achieved somewhat deficient to markedly deficient scores in tactile-kinesthetic-proprioceptive perception: complex; fine motor control; eye-hand coordination; orientation: space; visual perception: form discrimination and constancy; auditory constancy; linguistics input; integration: non-verbal and symbolic: tangible and abstract; and linguistics: verbal output.

Re-training was undertaken to correct the defects in tactile perception, fine motor control, eye-hand coordination, orientation in space, visual perception, and non-verbal integration. Douglas received training over a six-month period, four days a week for a half hour. The activities presented in Appendix C for training each of these areas were used. For example, cutaneous stimulation, resistive exercise, and activities for the identification of body parts were used to train the tactile function. Stencils for tracing, patterns, and worksheets were used for training fine motor control. Several functions were trained simultaneously such as the tactile, fine motor, and visual discrimination areas. Eye-hand coordination, spatial orientation, and non-verbal integration were trained later.

It is important to allow the child to master each series of activities in the sequence of a training pattern before going on to the next. Repetition and reinforcement offer the practice needed to accomplish the task. We have found from experience that it is more profitable to train certain functions before others since it appears that the development of adequacy in some of the higher level functions is dependent on the adequate development of preceding ones. The order in which the functions appear on the cognitive-perceptual-motor rating summary illustrates the preferred training order (see Appendix C).

Simultaneous training of several functions, however, is necessary and some functions appear to be more compatible in this respect than others. The tactile, gross motor, fine motor, orientation, visual, and auditory perception functions may be trained simultaneously and should be improved before the integration, linguistics, and memory functions are trained.

At the conclusion of Douglas' training he was retested on the Cognitive-Perceptual-Motor Battery. The before and after training scores are presented in Table 1.

Douglas continued to demonstrate some deficiencies in complex motor control, eye-hand coordination, and non-verbal integration; however, the increase in skill that he achieved in these areas as well as in tactile functions and spatial orientation appeared to help him specifically in improving his handwriting, increasing his ability to attend, and to lessen the confusion which accompanied his poor environmental orientation. He was able to chart his own progress by looking at his initial performance on certain tasks and comparing it with later performance. He began to set goals for himself such as learning to play

93

Function	Score before training	Score after training
Tactile-Kinesthetic Proprioceptive Perception		
Simple	AP	AP
Complex	SD	AP
Fine Motor Control		
Simple	SD	AP
Complex	SD-MD	SD
Gross Motor Coordination		
Eye Hand	MD	SD
Orientation		
Space	AP-SD	AP
Integration		
Non-verbal	MD	SD

Table 1. Scores before and after C-P-M Training

jacks (which was a current fad on the ward and a game he had been unable to play). With increased eye-hand coordination he was able to learn the game well enough to compete successfully with his peers. Douglas would also compete against his own previous performance on the worksheets and later on the puzzles.

In individual perception training many psychological problems which are manifested in the activity groups may also be seen, such as sibling rivalry and occasional lack of motivation. These are handled the same as in the group using anticipation, clarification, and limit-setting as well as other behavior management techniques.

In addition to training Douglas also received individual psychotherapy and milieu therapy.

Case Illustration 2

Matthew S., a nine and a half-year old, was referred to the clinic because of poor academic work with unwillingness or inability to do written work in school, and social withdrawal.

He was considered for the Cognitive-Perceptual-Motor Evaluation because of his reported academic difficulties and subsequent performance on achievement testing in the clinic school and his performance on psychological testing and on the Occupational Therapy Evaluation Battery, as well as his tendency to withdraw in stressful situations.

On the cognitive-motor evaluation, Matthew achieved somewhat to markedly deficient scores in fine motor control; eye-hand coordination; visual perception: shape; immediate rate memory: visual; immediate meaningful memory: auditory and visual; abstract symbolic integration; and non-verbal integration.

A coordinated training program was undertaken with Matthew in which the functions of fine motor control, eye-hand coordination, visual perception, and non-verbal integration were trained in occupational therapy while the memory functions and abstract symbolic integration were trained in special education. Regular periodic meetings were necessary to communicate progress and facilitate planning.

Matthew received one and a half hours of intensive individual training four days a week for six months. The activities used in training included geometric form stencils; graded patterns for tracing; Frostig worksheets; graded puzzles; materials such as flash cards with pictures, letters, and words; nursery rhymes and poems; thinking skills worksheets; and supplementary games.

At the conclusion of training Matthew demonstrated improvements in most of the areas he had received training in (see Table 2). However, continued deficiencies were demonstrated in fine motor control in complex situations, and in immediate rate memory of visual stimuli. Outstanding behavioral improvements associated with increased adequacy to perform in academic and other

Function	Score before training	Score after training
Fine Motor Control		
Simple	SD	AP
Complex	SD	SD
Gross Motor		
Eye Hand	SD	AP
Visual Perception		
Shape	SD	AP
Memory		
Immediate Rate Visual	SD	SD
Immediate Meaningful		
Auditory	SD	AP
Visual	SD	AP
Integration		
Non-verbal	SD	AP
Symbolic Abstract	MD	AP

Table 2. Scores before and after C-P-M Training

areas were noted in school, the ward, in O.T., R.T., and in psychotherapy in the form of more appropriate, spontaneous, outgoing behavior in social situations.

In planning cognitive-motor training for children assessment is of utmost importance. Further study both in the area of assessment and training techniques is indicated before more definitive conclusions can be drawn; however, the exclusion of this area from the handbook would be inappropriate even though our experience to date has been limited. Our results strongly suggest that such training should be included in residential treatment for emotionally disturbed children.

SUMMARY

This program has been designed to promote the development of ego functions to increase the child's ability to respond in an adaptive manner in his environment.

Disturbed children have been viewed as maladapted in areas of developmental skill, behavior, and the ability to relate to others. It is our assumption that these children can be helped to improve their functional ability, behavior functioning, and interpersonal interaction through systematically applied graded activities and relationships beginning at the child's level of developmental functioning.

It is not our intent to present this program as a rigidly designed cure-all for the problems of programming for children with emotional disturbances. It is presented as a model which considers the natural pattern of child development rationale. Flexibility must be expected in the application of these concepts to other settings. All aspects of this program have been tested for applicability in milieu treatment.

Appendix A:

Milieu Treatment Data

Pre-Admission Data Sheet*

Name _____ Age ____ Date admitted _____

Reason for admission:

Mother: Father:

Siblings: Other family or friends:

History prior to admission:

Likes   *Dislikes*   *Fears*

* The forms and outlines in this appendix are copies of actual forms used at Lafayette Clinic during the time this program was developed.

Pre-Admission Data Sheet (cont.)

Interview material:

Psychologicals: I.Q. _____

    General Comments:

School: Previous School: _____

          Chronological age grade placement: _____

          Actual grade placement: _____

          General Comments:

Cues for observations of ward behavior and nursing care plans:

Diagnostic Conference Outline

I. *Presentation of case*

   a. Identification of child, name, age, sex, chief complaints and present illness by resident
   b. Family history by social service
   c. Observations and evaluations
      1. Psychotherapy
      2. Psychology
      3. Nursing
      4. School
      5. O.T.
      6. R.T.

Reports from all departments except psychiatry due twenty-four hours before conference.

II. *Coordinated formulation based upon the presentation of the case*

   a. Diagnosis
   b. Statement of etiology
   c. Tentative impression of prognosis based on information currently available. This may be subject to change at time of progress conference in 8 weeks.

III. *General treatment plan in view of needs of the child and ultimate goals of treatment,* e.g., encourage acting-out in withdrawn children, discourage acting-out in antisocial children, limit-setting, separation from family, placement, work with parents if possible, return of child to home, working through core conflicts, basic problems of identify, low self-esteem, etc.

Children's Service Nursing Report

Patient's name: _____ Period covered: _____

Age: _____ Sex: _____

1. Behavior observations: _____

_____
_____
_____
_____
_____
_____
_____
_____
_____
_____
_____
_____
_____
_____
_____
_____
_____
_____
_____
_____
_____
_____
_____
_____
_____
_____
_____

Children's Service Nursing Report (cont.)

2. Favorite activities: _____

_____

_____

_____

_____

_____

_____

_____

3. Relationships: _____

_____

_____

_____

_____

_____

_____

4. Medications: _____

_____

_____

_____

5. Goals: _____

_____

_____

_____

_____

_____

*Special Education Diagnostic Report**
(outline)

Name: (last, first, M.I.)   Case number:

Age: Date of birth:

Chronological age grade placement:

A. *School history*

Give a brief summarization of the following: Name of schools attended, attendance record, failures, current grade placement and academic standing, behavioral description.

B. *Testing results and interpretations*

List all tests given, the scores or results, and the degree of retardation or acceleration. Discuss interpretation of test results in regard to the child's academic abilities and disabilities.

C. *School plan and goals*

State academic placement and goals based upon testing results, observations and other information.

D. *Academic performance*

Describe current functioning in all subject areas. Discuss progress, changes in functioning, and the results of specific techniques which have been attempted.

E. *Behavior and adjustment*

Give a detailed evaluation of the student's school behavior as you have observed him in class. Include attitudes toward school, motivation, self-concept, temper display (frequency), attention-seeking behavior, respect for routines, self-control, response to controls, attention span, frustration tolerance, reaction to frustration, affect, inappropriate behavior, anxiety, relationships,

---

* Distributed as follows:

original   —clinic record
1 copy   —therapist
2 copies —school file

Special Education Diagnostic Report (cont.)

(teacher-peer-group). Also include evidence of hostility, hyper-activity, ambivalence, manipulation, distractibility, withdrawal, antisocial behavior, dependency, provocative behavior, immaturity, and isolation as they relate to this particular student. Observational checklists should be used for this section.

F. *Summary and recommendations*

State current level of functioning, degree of acceleration or retardation, and prognosis for adjustment in other school settings.

(signed) _____
          Name
          Special Education Teacher
          Unit

(signed) _____
          Name, Supervisor
          Special Education

FORMULATION

The formulation may be defined as an educational diagnosis of the child's school difficulties, both academic and
behavioral since each applies. It is derived from a determina-
tion of the most relevant causative factors in the child's presenting problem as each either positively or negatively affects
his ability to function optimally in *all* aspects of the school
setting. These factors are the product of evaluations of the
child and examination of all the available information on his
past and present history as gained from the diagnostic conference.

The formulation serves several purposes. It is primarily
used as a basis on which to develop, expand, and revise the
original academic and educationally therapeutic goals and
plans for the child. These include placement, management,
and socialization. It is a general description of what our program has to offer each child and how it may be best adapted
to suit his needs. With those displaying few or none of their
psychiatric problems in the school situation, such evaluation
is equally important. The formulation also serves as a formal
means of keeping all teachers working with the same child
and informed of the plans for him, thus maintaining consistency in approach and efforts. Evaluation of the effect of
the established program is important and the formulation
also serves as a "yardstick" for measuring this in both academic and behavioral areas.

Special Education Formulation*
(outline)

A. Presenting problems

B. History (that which contributes to the emotional problem)
1. Family
   a. Parent(s) (surrogates)
   b. Siblings
2. School
   a. Placement
   b. Behavior
3. Peer relationships
4. Adult relationships

C. Evaluations
1. Academic achievement
2. Present family situation
3. Psychiatric evaluation
4. Psychological evaluation (I.Q. and projectives)
5. Occupational therapy
6. Recreational therapy
7. Behavior and interests
   a. School
   b. Other areas
8. Neurological

D. School placement and goals
1. Statement of plan and placement
2. Statement of goals
3. Reasons for #1 and #2 (based upon A, B, C)

(Signed) _____
          Name
          Special Education Teacher
          Unit

(Signed) _____
          Name, Supervisor
          Special Education

* Distributed as follows:

original —school file
1 copy —supervisor's file
1 copy —school file

Occupational Therapy Diagnostic Conference Report
(outline)

Occupational Therapy Report   Diagnostic Conference
Name: Date:
Age: Case No.:

I. Initial evaluation summary
II. O.T. plan and goals:
III. Placement: group and number of children
IV. Observations and further evaluation of child's functioning to include:
 a. *Interest:* toward activities, toward O.T., particular interest.
 b. *Work habits and performance:* established, poorly, well, improving, use of time. Evaluation of skills, improvement. Manner of working. Motivation. Attention span. Distractibility. Frustration tolerance; reaction to frustration—what frustrates him. Sharing ability; tools and materials, attention of the therapist.
 c. *Socialization and relationships:* social skills, does he verbalize spontaneously with peers? Adults? Topics of conversations. Does he interact with peers in activities? Does he relate to any one peer in particular? Does he relate to adults? Quality of relationship. Manner of relating.
 d. *Behavior:* overall behavior; description of most typical behavior—hostile, aggressive, dependent, independent, manipulative, withdrawn, hyperactive, distractible, teasing, provocative, rituals or mannerisms. Temper outburst—frequency, severity, cause for outbursts, what helps him over an outburst. Acting-out behavior-cause, frequency. Overly compliant behavior, etc.
V. Summary: current level of functioning, changes if any, areas in which continued work is needed.
VI. Formulation: based on treatment goals outlined by this conference. To be completed following the conference.

Recreational Therapy Activity Report
(outline)

           Doctor _____

Name _____Age ____File No. ____Ward _____
 Attendance:
 Activity:
 Attitude toward activity:
 Performance:
 Attitude toward self: Group: Therapist:
 Personal appearance:
 Anecdotic progress notes:
      Therapist _____Date: _____

Progress Conference Outline

I. *Review of case regarding changes.*
  a. *Identification of child,* etc. by resident with a brief 3 to 4 sentence summary of chief complaints and present illness.
  b. *Brief summary of family history and work with parents by Social Service* NOT TO EXCEED 5 MINUTES DURATION.
  c. Additional observations, response to treatment and re-evaluation also NOT TO EXCEED 5 MINUTES DURATION.

  1. Psychotherapy
  2. Psychology
  3. Nursing
  4. School
  5. O.T.
  6. R.T.

Reports from all departments except psychiatry due twenty-four hours before conference.

II. *Review of diagnosis and formulation made at diagnostic conference.*
III. *Review of general treatment plan, goals of treatment and prognosis.*
IV. *Statement of indicated changes in plans.* Based on #1. (Review of case)
V. *Ultimate disposition of case, e.g., continue in hospital, psychotherapy indicated for parents, continued social service case work with parents, discharge of patient to a placement setting, i.e., foster home, group placement, group setting, etc.*

Children's Service Nursing Report
(outline)

Patient's name ———————————Period covered ————

Age: ———————————————Sex: ——————————

  1. Behavior observations: ——————————————————

————————————————————————————

————————————————————————————

————————————————————————————

————————————————————————————

————————————————————————————

Children's Service Nursing Report (cont.)

2. Favorite activities: _____

_____

_____

_____

_____

_____

_____

_____

3. Relationships: _____

_____

_____

_____

_____

_____

_____

4. Medication: _____

_____

_____

_____

_____

_____

5. Goals: _____

_____

_____

_____

Special Education Progress Conference Report*
(outline)

Name: (last, first, M.I.)   Age: Case Number:
Chronological age grade placement:

A. *School plan*
   State placement and goals formulated as a result of the
   Diagnostic Conference. Describe techniques used for
   achieving goals.
B. *Academic performance*
   Report the grade level at which the child is functioning
   in each subject area. Include the progress (or lack of progress) and changes in the student in school since the last
   conference. Be specific and give examples.
C. *Behavior and adjustment*
   Report the progress (or lack of progress), changes, or differences in the student's classroom behavior as you have
   recorded them in the weekly logs and observational checklists.
   This section should include all the same information as
   in Part D.
D. *Summary and recommendations*
   State current level of functioning, degree of acceleration
   or retardation, and prognosis for adjustment in other
   school settings.

(signed) _____
         Name
         Special Education Teacher
         Unit
(signed) _____
         Name, Supervisor
         Special Education

* Distributed as follows:
   original —clinical record
   1 copy   —therapist
   1 copy   —school file

Occupational Therapy Progress Conference Report
(outline)

Occupational Therapy Report   Progress Conference

Name: Date:

Age: Case No.:

I. *Attends O.T. in:* Name the group and number of children.
II. O.T. Plan: state goals and attitudes formulated as a result of the diagnostic conference and the means used to achieve them.
III. Observations and changes in child's functioning in areas of:
   a. *Interest:* toward activities, toward O.T., particular interest.
   b. *Work Habits and performance:* established, poorly, well, improving, use of time. Evaluation of skills, improvement. Manner of working. Motivation. Attention span. Distractibility. Frustration tolerance; reaction to frustration—what frustrates him. Sharing ability; tools and materials, attention of the therapist.
   c. *Socialization and relationships:* social skills, does he verbalize spontaneously with peers? Adults? Topics of conversations. Does he interact with peers in activities? Does he relate to any one peer in particular? Does he relate to adults? Quality of relationship. Manner of relating.
   d. *Behavior:* overall behavior; description of most typical behavior—hostile, aggressive, dependent, independent, manipulative, withdrawn, hyperactive, distractible, teasing, provocative, rituals or mannerisms. Temper outburst—frequency, severity, cause for outbursts, what helps him over an outburst. Acting-out behavior-cause, frequency. Overly-compliant behavior, etc.
IV. Summary: current level of functioning, changes if any, areas in which continued work is indicated.
V. Continuing O.T. Plan: based on results of this conference.

Recreational Therapy Activity Report
(outline)

Doctor _____

Name _____Age ____File No. ____ Ward _____

Attendance:
Activity:
Attitude toward activity:
Performance:
Attitude toward self: Group: Therapist:
Personal appearance:
Anecdotic progress notes:

Therapist _____Date: _____

Appendix B:

Evaluation Battery

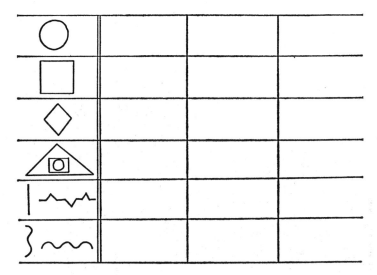

Figure 1. L-R Fine Motor Control Test

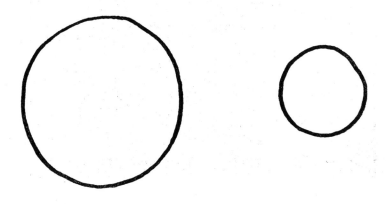

Figure 2. Circle Patterns for Eye-Hand Coordination Test

117

Figure 3. Jigsaw Puzzle

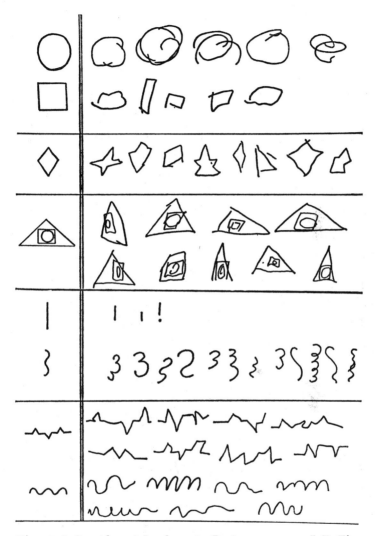

Figure 4. Samples of Inadequate Performance on L-R Fine Motor Control Test

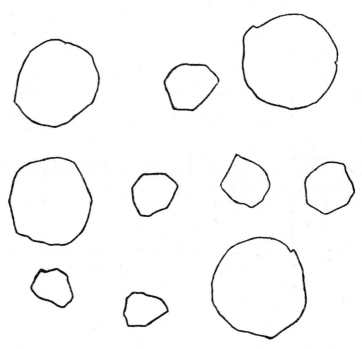

Figure 5. Samples of Inadequate Performance on Eye-Hand Coordination Test

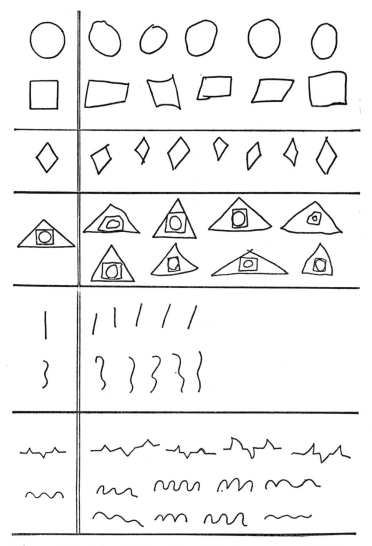

Figure 6. Samples of Transitional Performance on L-R Fine Motor Control Test

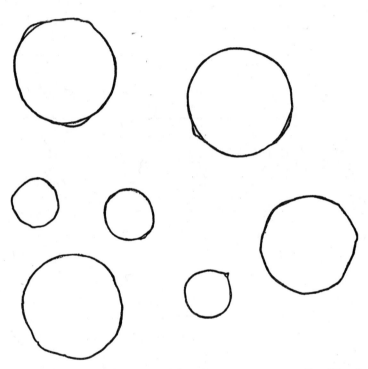

Figure 7. Samples of Transitional Performance on Eye-Hand Coordination Test

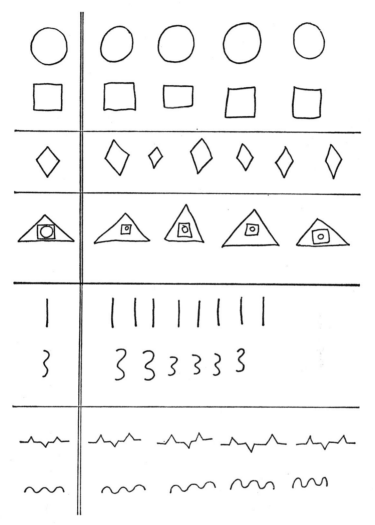

Figure 8. Samples of Adequate Performance on L-R Fine Motor Control Test

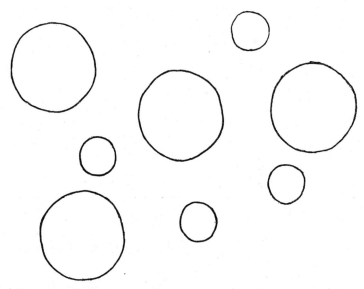

Figure 9. Samples of Adequate Performance on Eye-Hand Coordination Test

Observations	1 = Inadequate	2 = Transitional	3 = Adequate
Time to complete puzzle	10 minutes or more	8–10 minutes	7 minutes or less
Organization and method used to complete	No organization. Trial & error	Use of trial & error and visual clues	Use of boundaries, corners, visual clues, etc. to organize

Figure 10. Scoring Criteria for Puzzle

Observations	1 = Inadequate	2 = Transitional	3 = Adequate
Attention span	Restless. Unable to complete tasks assigned	Some restlessness but able to complete tasks assigned	Adequate for each task. Appropriate to situation
Ability to concentrate	Easily distracted by objects in the environment, inner thoughts, etc.	Some distraction, will resume task independently. Is easily recalled	Attends to activity without distraction
Ability to follow verbal directions	Unable to do what is asked. Does what is asked in a way that demonstrates lack of understanding. Will not follow directions	Does what is asked but needs repeat of directions, may ask questions about directions while doing activity	Does what is asked with no questions or need to have directions repeated
Degree of motor activity	Increased or decreased motor activity		Appropriately spontaneous
Relatedness to therapist	Unrelating. Responds only when questioned. Is overly responsive		Appropriately spontaneous
Dependence-independence	Dependent on therapist for approval. Seeks help. Does not seek help	Seeks help initially but can work independently	Works independently. Seems self-confident
Affect & mood	Flattened. Inappropriate to the situation		Appropriate to situation

Figure 11. Scoring Criteria for Behavioral Observations

Name: Date:
Age: Testing No.:

Skills				Child's Score	Maximum Score
Fine motor control					15
Eye-hand coordination	Shape distortion due to uneven cutting—1	Recognizable shape, lack of smoothness—2	Smoothness and accuracy of form—3		3
Integration	Time: More than 10 minutes —1	8–10 minutes—2	Less than 8 minutes—3		3
	No organization, trial and error—1	Predominant use of trial and error with visual clues—2	Predominant use of boundaries, corners, visual clues etc. to organize—3		3
Total					24
Behavior	Where a choice is indicated, underline the appropriate behavior response.				
Attention span	Restless. Unable to complete tasks assigned—1	Some restlessness but able to complete tasks assigned—2	Adequate for each task. Appropriate to situation—3		3

1 = Inadequate   2 = Transitional   3 = Adequate

*Figure 12. Score Sheet for O.T. Evaluation Battery
(Children 6–12)*

				Child's Score	Maximum Score
Concentration	Easily distracted by objects in the environment, inner thoughts, etc.—1	Some distraction, will resume task independently. Is easily recalled—2	Attends to activity without distraction —3		3
Follow directions	Unable to do what is asked. Does what is asked in a way that demonstrates lack of understanding. Will not follow directions—1	Does what is asked but needs repeat of directions, may ask questions about directions while doing the activity—2	Does what is asked with no questions or need to have questions repeated—3		3
Motor activity	Increased or decreased motor activity—1		Appropriately spontaneous—3		3
Total					12
Relatedness	Unrelating. Responds only when questioned. Is overly responsive —1		Appropriately spontaneous—3		3

Figure 12. (cont.)

				Child's Score	Maximum Score
Dependence-Independence	Dependent on therapist for approval. Seeks help. Does not seek help —1	Seeks help initially but can work independently —2	Works independently. Seems self-confident —3		3
Affect & mood	Flattened. Inappropriate to situation —1		Appropriate to situation—3		3
Total					9

Figure 12. (cont.)

Appendix C:

*Cognitive-Perceptual-Motor Manual
and Rating Summary*

Manual of Cognitive-Perceptual-Motor Functions
(contains screening battery only*)

Function	Definition	Assessment Techniques	Training Techniques
1. Tactile-kinesthetic-proprioceptive perception	Central response to stimuli presented only to tactual senses—inferred from behavior response	Tactile-kinesthetic-proprioceptive perception test	Tactile-kinesthetic-proprioceptive sequence which includes cutaneous stimulation, passive and resistive exercise Identification of body parts, etc. Identification of objects by touch with sight occluded Assembling simple puzzles with sight occluded Sand play
2. Fine motor control	Control of fine motor movements in simple and complex situations	Simple: Frostig Complex: Bender-Gestalt	Tracing beginning with geometric form stencils, geometric patterns, through animal form patterns Visual motor worksheets Tracing worksheets Coloring worksheets
3. Gross motor coordination	Coordination of large muscles in purposeful manner, including eye-hand coordination and coordination of extremities		

* The comprehensive battery contains additional assessment techniques.

a. Eye-hand	Ability to use muscles to perform coordinated tasks such as cutting	Frostig I	Eye exercises Frostig worksheets Visual motor worksheets Copying worksheets Visual motor worksheets Cutting out objects from magazines, etc. Suppl.: Jacks, ringtoss, pegboard, sewing cards
b. Extremities	Smooth functioning of arms and legs in walking	Kephart Perceptual Survey	Bouncing a ball, beachball, two hands, dominant hand. Basketball, two hands, dominant hand. Tennis ball, dominant hand Catching Roll ball to child sitting on the floor Have child bounce a balloon in the air, keeping it aloft Throw balloon to child, keep aloft between you Beach ball Volley ball Soft ball Throwing a ball Throwing a ball in a Wastebasket Horseshoes

Manual (cont.)

Function	Definition	Assessment Techniques	Training Techniques
Gross motor coordination (cont.)			Ringtoss
			Bean Bag throw
			Dart throw
			Shooting baskets
			Throwing a ball at a wall target
			Batting a ball
			Hit a ball on a stationary string with a paddle
			Hit ball on a moving string with a paddle
			Hit ball on a moving string with a bat
			Throw ball to child at short distance, let child use paddle. After success use bat. Increase distance
			Walk on a line
			Walking beam
			Trampoline
			Jumping rope, simple & complex
			Kick ball from a stationary position
			(Soccer ball to volleyball)
			Kick ball while being rolled to him

			Kick football held in own hands
4. Orientation	Awareness of relationships between the child and events and objects in the environment, along the dimensions of time, space, and size		
a. Space		Frostig New York Test of Arithmetical Meanings Level I, Test I; Level II, Test I Lee Clark Test III (11, 14, 19) Orientation Questionnaire	Physical Exercises: Rolling over Crawling Walk on a line Walk on balance board Identifying body parts using neuromuscular facilitation techniques Human figure puzzles Frostig worksheets Drill in left-right using visual discrimination worksheets Suppl.: Magnet board Hokey Pokey Simon Says
b. Size		Orientation Questionnaire NYTA items Lee Clark Test III (9, 10, 12)	Frostig worksheets Suppl.: Magnet board

Manual (cont.)

Function	Definition	Assessment Techniques	Training Techniques
5. Visual perception	Central response to visual stimulus, inferred from verbal or motor response		
a. Discrimination	Recognition of similarities and differences when the stimuli are increasingly similar checked along various visual dimensions, including form, size, and space	Form: Lee Clark, Test I (S) Test IV Frostig Size: Lafayette Clinic Test Space: Monroe Reading Apt., Vis. Test I	Flash cards (objects, letters, numbers, words) Visual discrimination worksheets Frostig worksheets Suppl.: Magnet board
b. Constancy	Holding of a symbolic representation of a form, in both simple and complex stimulus situations	Frostig Durrell Visual Memory of Words Durrell Visual Memory of Letters (beginning and intermediate)	Frostig worksheets Visual discrimination worksheets for similarities covering up stimulus object
6. Auditory perception	Central response to auditory stimulus		
a. Discrimination	Recognition of similarity and difference between auditorily presented stimuli, not musical sounds but rather language symbols	Sound Discrimination Test Wepman Test	Listening exercises Nursery rhymes Poems Tape-recorded "worksheets" Paired word lists Suppl.: Games

b. Constancy	Holding of a memory of an auditory stimulus and to recognize it among competing stimuli	Lafayette Clinic Auditory Perceptual Constancy Test	Reading readiness and phonics materials Rhyming worksheets
7. Orientation time	(See item #3)	Orientation Questionnaire	Problems in before, after, now, & later Worksheets Season Coloring sheets Play Calendar Suppl.: Play clock Tell-time Lotto
8. Linguistics input	Ability to understand what is said through gestures and words	Illinois Test of Psycholinguistic Abilities Gates Primary Reading Test, Type PPR, Form I	Action rhythms record Out-of-doors record Oral commands Written commands
9. Memory	Memory for digits or arbitrary, unrelated series of items, to be recalled immediately, using both visual and auditory presentations	Visual: Monroe Visual Test III Auditory:	Visual: flash cards—pictures, letters, words, phrases Auditory: naming letters, numbers, and words
b. Immediate meaningful	Recall of rote details, content and meaning immediately after presentation	Monroe Language Test III—Visual Monroe Reading Aptitude Auditory Test III Durrell Listening Comprehension	Nursery rhymes Sentences Poems Paragraphs Stories and events
c. Delayed rote	Recall of items after time lapse	Detroit Reading Readiness V	Same as for immediate rote but with a time lapse

Manual (cont.)

Function	Definition	Assessment Techniques	Training Techniques
10. Integration a. Non-verbal	Ability to combine discreet stimuli into meaningful whole	Jigsaw puzzle	Graded puzzles Frostig worksheets Visual discrimination worksheets Visual motor worksheets
b. Symbolic	Ability to abstract qualities or meanings from stimuli and to form constructs transferable from situation to situation, using materials that are tangible, abstract, and numerical	Tangible: Concept Section, ITPA, CTM, 6 and 7 Abstract: Monroe Language Test II, Lafayette Clinic Test	Verbal: thinking skills worksheets Independent activities worksheets Suppl.: Who Gets It game Play Store game Play House game Numerical: Blocks & objects Number readiness worksheets Arithmetic readiness workbooks Suppl.: Number readiness games

11. Linguistics output	Ability to communicate and express ideas through language	Verbal: ITPA Non-Verbal: ITPA	Naming objects See Quees puzzle Series 4 & 12 Picture books Telling endings to stories Telling simple to complex stories and events
12. Integration Inferential Reasoning	Abstraction of meaning from oral material implied not explicit	Gates Reading Survey Grades 3–10, Form I (speed)	Reading thinking skills worksheets
Dominance	Establishment of preferred hand, foot, and eye	Harris Test	

Cognitive-Perceptual-Motor Rating Summary

Name _____ Date _____

Age _____ Birthdate _____ Sex ____

I.Q.: V _____ P _____ FS _____ Other _____

Date of admission _____ Testing _____

Date of discharge _____ Length of stay _____

Examiner _____

1. Tactile-kinesthetic-
   proprioceptive perception
   Simple _____
   Complex _____
2. Fine motor control
   Simple _____
   Complex _____
3. Gross motor coordination
   a. Eye-Hand _____
   b. Extremities _____
4. Orientation
   a. Space _____
   b. Size _____
5. Visual perception
   a. Discrimination
      Form _____
      Size _____
      Shape _____
   b. Constancy _____
6. Auditory perception
   a. Discrimination _____
   b. Constancy _____
7. Orientation
   Time _____
8. Linguistics
   Input _____
Comments:

9. Memory
   a. Immediate rote
      Visual _____
      Auditory _____
   b. Immediate meaningful
      Visual _____
      Auditory _____
   c. Delayed Rote _____
10. Integration
    a. Non-verbal _____
    b. Symbolic _____
       Tangible _____
       Abstract _____
    c. Number _____
11. Linguistics
    Output
    Verbal _____
    Non-verbal _____
12. Integration
    Inferential
    Reasoning _____

Dominance
   Established right _____
   Established left _____
   Handedness _____
   Footedness _____
   Eyeness _____

Appendix D:

References and Resources

Books and Pamphlets

Cherry, Raymond. *General Leathercraft*. McKnight and Mc-Knight Publ. Co., Bloomington, Ill.

Coleman, Gerry, Marguerite Koenig, and Edna Berry. *Copper Enameling*. Gick Enterprises, Inglewood, Cal.

Diller, Mary Blac. *Drawing for Young Artists*. Pitman Publishing Corp., New York.

Epps, Helen O., Gertrude B. McCammon, and Queen D. Simmons. *Teaching Devices for Children with Impaired Learning*. Parents Volunteer Association of the Columbus State School, Inc., Columbus.

Foster, Walter. *Oil Painting*. Foster Art Service, Inc., Laguna Beach, Cal.

Goblirsch, Margaret and Katerine M. Daly. *Classroom Papercraft Projects and Patterns*. Fearn Publishers, Inc., San Francisco.

Leeming, Joseph. *Fun With Paper*. J. B. Lippincott Co., Philadelphia.

McCall's Golden Do-It-Book. Golden Press, New York.

Metal Decorating with Stamp-Engraving and Etching. Pacific Arts and Crafts, Inglewood.

Moseley, Spencer, Pauline Johnson, and Hazel Loenig. *Crafts, Design.* Wadsworth Publishing Co., Inc., Belmont, Cal.

Pauli, Anna and Margaret S. Mitzit. *Paper Figures.* Charles A. Bennett, Co., Inc., Peoria, Ill.

Richmond, Leonard. *Oil Painting.* Pitman Publishing Co., New York.

Silk Screen and Block Printing. Pacific Arts and Crafts, Inglewood.

Soong, Maying. *The Art of Chinese Paper Folding.* Harcourt, Brace & World, Inc., New York.

Thompson, Seeley. *Activities in Ceramics.* McKnight and McKnight Publ. Co., Bloomington.

Thompson, Thomas E., *Enameling on Copper and other Metals.* Thomas C. Thompson Co., Highland Park, Ill.

Materials and Sources

Creative Playthings, Inc., Princeton Road, Cranbury, N.J.

The Frostig Program for the Development of Visual Perception by Marianne Frostig and David Horne, Follett Publishing Company, Chicago (a program for training skills in perception of position in space, perception of spatial relationships, perceptual constancy, visual motor coordination, and figure-ground perception).

My World of Art Series, Chicago.

Our Book Series, Chicago (pre-printed masters for worksheets).

Reading Fundamentals Program by Ethel C. Maney, Continental Press, Inc., Elizabethtown, Pa. (pre-printed masters for training visual motor skills, visual discrimination skills, symbolic integration skills, auditory discrimination skills, number skills, and others).

The Slingerland Kit by Beth M. Slingerland and Anna Gillingham, Educators Publishing Service, Inc., Cambridge, Mass.

Tandy Leather Co., Fort Worth, Texas (instruction sheets are available with kits).

Whitman Publishing Co., Racine, Wis. (materials such as activity books, coloring books, and dot-to-dot number picture books).

Selected Bibliography

Books

Allen, Fred H. *Psychotherapy with Children.* New York, 1942.

Bender, Lauretta. *Aggression, Hostility and Anxiety* Springfield, 1953.

————. *Child Psychiatric Techniques.* Springfield, 1952.

————. *Psychopathology of Children With Organic Brain Disorders.* Springfield, 1956.

Berkowitz, R. P. and E. Rothman. *The Disturbed Child.* New York, 1961.

Bettleheim, Bruno. *The Informed Heart.* Glencoe, 1960.

Cummings, John and Elaine. *Ego and Milieu.* New York, 1962.

Dixon, Wilfred and Frank J. Massey. *Introduction to Statistical Analysis.* New York, 1957.

Erikson, Erik. *Childhood and Society.* New York, 1950.

Fidler, Gail and Jay. *Occupational Therapy: A Communication Process in Psychiatry.* New York, 1963.

Gesell, A. L. *Infant and Child in the Culture of Today.* New York, 1946.

―――. *The Child from Five to Ten.* New York, 1946.

―――. *The First Five Years of Life.* New York, 1940.

Good, Carter V., and Douglas E. Scates. *Methods of Research.* New York, 1954.

Hartmann, Heinz. *Ego Psychology and the Problem of Adaptation.* New York, 1960.

Hebb, D. O. *The Organization of Behavior.* New York, 1949.

Hunt, J. McV. *Intelligence and Experience.* New York, 1961.

Kephart, Newell C. *The Slow Learner in the Classroom.* Columbus, 1960.

Lippman, Hyman S. *Treatment of the Child in Emotional Conflict.* New York, 1962.

Lowenfeld, Vikter. *Creative and Mental Growth.* New York, 1956.

Noyes, Arthur P. and Lawrence C. Kolb. *Modern Clinical Psychiatry.* 6th ed.; Philadelphia, 1960.

Piaget, Jean. *The Construction of Reality in the Child.* New York, 1954.

―――. *The Language and Thought of the Child.* New York, 1926.

―――. *The Origins of Intelligence in Children.* New York, 1952.

Rambusch, Nancy M. *Learning How to Learn: An American Approach to Montessori.* Baltimore, 1962.

Redl, Fritz and David Wineman. *Children Who Hate.* Glencoe, 1952.

―――. *Controls From Within.* Glencoe, 1952.

Schad, Carol J. and Anne T. Dally. *Occupational Therapy in Pediatrics.* Dubuque, 1959.

Scott, John Paul. *Aggression.* Chicago, 1958.

Slavson, S. R. *An Introduction to Group Therapy.* New York, 1944.

143

Strauss, Alfred H. and Laura E. Lehtinen. *Psychopathology and Education of the Brain-Injured Child.* New York, 1947.

Williams, Richard. *The Prevention of Disability in Mental Disorder.* Washington, 1958.

West, Wilma. *Changing Concepts in Psychiatric Occupational Therapy.* New York, 1956.

Articles

Ayres, A. Jean. "Development of Perceptual-Motor Abilities: A Theoretical Basis for Treatment of Dysfunction." *American Journal of Occupational Therapy,* XVII (1963), 221–25.

———. "Tactile Functions." *American Journal of Occupational Therapy,* XVIII (1964), 6–11.

———. "The Visual Motor Function." *American Journal of Occupational Therapy* XII (1958), 130–38.

Beck, Gayle R., et al. "Educational Aspects of Cognitive-Perceptual-Motor Deficits in Emotionally Disturbed Children." *Psychology in the Schools,* II (July 1965), 233–38.

Bettleheim, Bruno and Emmy Sylvester. "A Therapeutic Milieu." *Journal of Orthopsychiatry,* XVIII (1948), 191–206.

Braun, Jean S., et al. "Cognitive-Perceptual-Motor Functions in Children—A Suggested Change in Approach." *Journal of School Psychology,* III (Spring 1965), 13–17.

Llorens, Lela A. "Psychological Tests in Planning Therapy Goals." *American Journal of Occupational Therapy,* XIV, (1960), 243–46.

Llorens, Lela A., and Stuart P. Bernstein. "Finger-painting with an Obsessive-Compulsive Organically Brain-Damaged Child." *American Journal of Occupational Therapy,* XVII (1963), 120–21.

Llorens, Lela A., and Eli Z. Rubin. "Directed Activity Program for Disturbed Children." *American Journal of Occupational Therapy,* XVI (1962), 287–90.

———. "Occupational Therapy is Therapeutic: A Research Study with Emotionally Disturbed Children." *Proceedings of the Conference of the American Occoupational Therapy Association.* New York, 1961.

Llorens, Lela A. et al. "Training in Cognitive-Perceptual-Motor Functions: A Preliminary Report." *American Journal of Occupational Therapy*, XVIII (1964), 202–7.

Llorens, Lela A. and Gregory G. Young. "Finger-painting for the Hostile Child." *American Journal of Occupational Therapy*, XIV (1960), 306–7.

Rachman, S. and C. G. Costello. "The Aetiology and Treatment of Children's Phobias: A Review." *American Journal of Psychiatry*, CXVIII (1961), 97–105.

Rubin, Eli Z. "Secondary Emotional Disorders in Children with Perceptual-Motor Dysfunction." *Journal of Orthopsychiatry*, XXXIV (1964), 296–97.

Weston, Donald L. "Dimensions in Crafts." *American Journal of Occupational Therapy*, XV (1961), 1–5.

———. "Therapeutic Crafts." *American Journal of Occupational Therapy*, XIV (1960), 121, 122, 133.

Unpublished Material

Azima, Fern. Workshop and lecture notes.

Cobb, Joan. "A Structured, Graded Activity Program in Occupational Therapy."

Fairman, Carl W. "Adjunctive Therapy for Children." Unpublished study conducted at Parsons State Hospital and Training Center, Parsons, Kansas.

Frostig, Marianne. "Perceptual Ability and School Adjustment in Kindergarten and Primary Grades." Paper presented at the December meeting of the California State Psychological Association, Los Angeles, 1961.

———. "Visual Perception in the Brain-Injured Child." Manuscript accepted for publication by the *American Journal of Orthopsychiatry*.

The Lafayette Clinic Special Education Program.

145

Index

The manuscript was edited by R. H. Tennenhouse. The book was designed by Joanne E. Colman. The text typeface is Mergenthaler's Linotype Baskerville. The display face is Venus Bold Extended designed by Bauer Type Foundry, 1907–13.

The book is printed on *Warren's 1854 Text* and bound in *Riegal's Carolina Cover*. Manufactured in the United States of America.

Lela A. Llorens is head of the Division of Occupational Therapy, Lafayette Clinic, Detroit, and an instructor in occupational therapy, Wayne State University.

Eli Z. Rubin is head of the Division of Psychology, Lafayette Clinic, and associate professor of psychology, Wayne State University.